THE COURAGE TO HOPE

The Roots for a New Vision and the Calling of the Church in Africa

SAMUEL KOBIA

THE COURAGE TO HOPE
The Roots for a New Vision and the
Calling of the Church in Africa

Risk
BOOK SERIES

WCC Publications, Geneva

Cover design: Chaz Maviyane-Davies
The cover illustration is adapted from the backdrop designed by
Chaz Maviyane-Davies for the Africa plenary, "A Journey of
Hope", at the WCC's eighth assembly in Harare, December 1998

ISBN 2-8254-1388-7

© 2003, WCC Publications, World Council of Churches
150 route de Ferney, P.O. Box 2100
1211 Geneva 2, Switzerland
Web site: http://www.wcc-coe.org

No. 102 in the Risk Book Series

Printed in Switzerland

Table of Contents

Foreword

A new spirit is manifesting itself in Africa. After forty years, the former Organization of African Unity has been transformed into the African Union. Shortly afterwards, the New Partnership for Africa's Development (NEPAD) was publicly initiated. These two projects demonstrated the will among a new generation of African leaders to act together in shaping the future of Africa. While questions may and should be raised regarding the viability of this new political vision, it constitutes a challenge to the churches and the ecumenical movement in Africa.

As early as 1992, the late Aaron Tolen, then president of the World Council of Churches (WCC) from Africa, challenged the ecumenical community "to look at Africa with new eyes". This meant, he said, to go beyond both the "liberation" and "development" discourses and to engage in "reconstruction" of Africa, drawing on its own moral and spiritual resources. Responding to this appeal, churches and ecumenical organizations in Africa, together with their partners overseas, began to engage in a process of discernment facilitated by the WCC. It culminated in a solemn covenant of African participants and those of African descent at the Harare assembly of the WCC in 1998, taking as its motto "A Journey of Hope for Africa".

Sam Kobia, the author of this book, has been one of the key actors in this process, providing both inspiration, orientation and coordination. As general secretary of the National Council of Churches in Kenya during the years of struggle for true democracy in his country, he developed decisive convictions about the calling of the church and its role in the reconstruction of Africa. Since 1998, he has been part of the staff leadership of the WCC, bringing his insights and commitments to bear on the worldwide ecumenical efforts to accompany the African churches in this process of spiritual discernment and empowerment for shaping the future of the continent and its people. The present book, the fruit of an extended study leave, intentionally echoes in its title the motif of the "journey of hope". Taking his clue from Paul Tillich's interpretation of Christian faith as "the courage to be", Sam Kobia translates Tillich's philosophical approach into the terms of that moral universe which continues to shape African life in community. Daring to hope against all odds is the ethical dimension of courage. Thus, "the objective of this book is to motivate Africans to be open to the future".

A new vision for Africa's future that is not to remain a pure utopia must be rooted in an effort of re-membering the past and in a critical assessment of the present. There is overwhelming evidence that Africa, the "forgotten continent" of today, was the birthplace and the original home of the human race. African cultures have preserved the consciousness of a moral universe which sustains the integrity of life in community. Centuries of slavery and colonialism have not been able to destroy this memory which today, following the end of colonial alienation, can become the source of reaffirming African identity as "being in relationship".

After reviewing the emergence and the early expressions of the vision of pan-Africanism, the book offers a critical assessment of the present with an analysis of the nation-state model imposed on Africa by colonial powers. While conventional approaches to the African dilemma focus exclusively on the features of economic (under-)development, Kobia with his analysis penetrates to the structural and spiritual roots of the problem. He shows that the lack of legitimacy afflicting public institutions in Africa and their continuous misappropriation for private gain is an inheritance from the period of colonial rule and its forms of governance. The combined impact of modernization and globalization has aggravated this condition.

What is needed, therefore, is an ethical reconstruction of the state as a public institution whose legitimacy is based on its accountability to the people and their needs. Such reconstruction needs to be based on the ethical and spiritual affirmation of human dignity and of the sanctity of life. Neither the traditional discourses of "liberation" or "development" nor the propagation of an "African renaissance" is able to achieve the fundamental paradigm shift away from the dominance of market values and the struggles around "ethnicity" towards a recovery of the communitarian ethic of African tradition.

This ethical imperative clarifies the vocation of the churches and the ecumenical community in Africa. A brief review of the developments over these past forty years shows that neither the All Africa Conference of Churches nor the churches themselves have been able to overcome their dependency on the structural models and the support provided by Northern partners. This weakens their voice in calling those in public offices to accountability. The need for a reorientation and a new awareness of the calling of the churches becomes urgent in view of the challenge of the HIV/AIDS pandemic. It is here that the courage to hope needs to find expression as an affirmation of life even in the face of death, and the churches as communities of the resurrection need to become "sanctuaries of life" for a community overcome by despair. Drawing on recent ecumenical reflections focusing on a "theology of life" and the need for providing "ecumenical space", Sam Kobia further develops the moral and spiritual foundations for his new vision for Africa.

This book is the result of many years of struggle within the WCC in an effort to come to terms with the dilemmas of Africa. It shows the complexity of the challenge and does not pretend to have found the comprehensive solution. But above all, it is a passionate and at times even an angry affirmation of African identity based on the deep conviction that Africa has the moral and spiritual resources for shaping a future that will provide life in dignity and sustainable community for all people. For all those who are committed to the reconstruction of Africa, this book will be an invaluable source of inspiration and encouragement.

July 2003   KONRAD RAISER
General Secretary of the
World Council of Churches

Preface

May the origin of all things, the absolute holy ground, the sole and whole explanation of the universe, and the source of all existence, whose name is spoken in many languages of the ancient people, bless Africa and her children.

It is my wish that the opening of these pages will bring new understanding and not seal the lips of the sages, for words once spoken and written shall remain inscribed in the tablets of history. Africa shall arise from her tired dreams and nightmares. This will not be the triumph of yet another continental empire, but the regaining of human dignity and the restoration of institutions of affection that will lead to the rebuilding of communities in which the value of the human person transcends the logic of the market. The millions of children in Africa, including those who today are orphaned due to the scourge of HIV/AIDS and live without basic resources of life and education, are the bearers of the burden of history for the continent. While under the reign of dysfunctional institutions and poor governance, there shall emerge among them a new generation of resilient leadership with fierce commitment to a new future. Africa must rise to the occasion to rebuild confidence among her sons and daughters and equip them with new instruments of discernment and understanding of reality.

Africa must awaken and be restored to her place of destiny. But that will happen only with the rekindling of community spirit and adherence to the values of dignity and participation in public matters and social responsibility.

The church in her calling to be a custodian of justice and peace, with her enormous social capital and capacity, must speak in unison. She must lead by example and accompany the poor and the weak with love and truth. Amid the ideological confusion and chaos in global economies, Africa must re-examine her priorities in the interest of her people's welfare. The African people must know and have the authority to challenge the power of the state, especially when it ceases to serve their needs and aspirations. And then without fear, but with the *courage to hope,* a new Africa will be reborn and behold! her people will *rejoice in hope.*

Acknowledgments

Most of the issues and themes explored in this publication were organized and drafted during my sabbatical as a Fellow at the Center for the Study of Values in Public Life (CSVPL), Divinity School, Harvard University. I would like to thank Konrad Raiser, general secretary of the World Council of Churches, for his encouragement and for granting the study leave. I am grateful to George Todd, a friend and former colleague, and to Harvey Cox, who were both instrumental in my choice of the CSVPL as the place for my study leave. While at the Center, I had regular discussions with a small group of African scholars and students from colleges and universities in the Boston area. I had even more in-depth discussions with Nicholas Otieno of Yale University whose views I considered to represent the mind of younger African scholars. I thank him for his valuable comments on earlier drafts. Special thanks are owed to the CSVPL, particularly to Brent Coffin, the executive director, and to Nancy Nienhuis who facilitated luncheon forums for discussion with my other Fellows.

At the end of my sabbatical, an excellent opportunity arose to conduct a reality check of my views. This occasion was provided by the Nairobi Peace Initiatives-Africa which sponsored a series of seminars and a public lecture in Nairobi. I wish to thank NPI-A and in particular Kabiru Kinyanjui, the chairman of the board, and George Wachira, the director. The general secretary of the National Council of Churches in Kenya, Mutava Musyimi, organized and sent very useful data which I used as primary sources of information. To augment primary data, I needed further information which my colleague Catherine Christ-Taha found on the internet and in the library of the WCC in Geneva. She also typed the manuscript, for which I particularly wish to thank her.

The love, encouragement and understanding of my wife Ruth and my children Kaburo, Nkatha, Mwenda and Mutua sustained my spirit to work. It is to them that I dedicate this book.

1. Introduction

As you press on for justice, be sure to move with dignity and discipline, using only the weapon of love. Let no man pull you so low as to hate him. Always avoid violence. If you succumb to the temptation of using violence in your struggle, unborn generations will be the recipients of a long and desolate night of bitterness, and your chief legacy to the future will be an endless reign of meaningless chaos.

Martin Luther King, 6 Nov. 1956

The ecumenical movement is ever exploring new frontiers of unity, even as it is being refined and redefined in the constant engagement of humanity with the divine. In the contemporary quest for unity, the most crucial and critical aspect of this engagement is grounded in a vision of life as a web of reciprocal relationships by which human beings find themselves interconnected with one another and with the rest of creation. Unity is predicated not so much on the process of historical development as on the relational nature of the one household of life.

Paul Tillich, a 20th-century Protestant theologian, considered the causes of human estrangement. He concluded that our alienation from one another and from God stems in part from the fact that living beings naturally strive for space. This condition is a consequence of the spatial character of finite being, yet no finite being possesses a space which is definitely its own. Every finite, living being faces losing what space it has, or might have had, because it is a pilgrim and sojourner on this earth. For human creatures, conscious of this, the question of meaning will inevitably arise.

In his book *The Courage To Be*, Paul Tillich presented Christian faith as the authentic, correlative response to the predicament of existence as expressed in human anxiety. So the corollary to finitude is shown to be the dimension of God as Creator, while the endless search for meaning is resolved by the Logos, that divine word or principle of order by which God brought all life into being (John 1:1). The philosophy of being, or "ontology", provides Tillich with an entry point in addressing questions of meaning, but it is theology that provides the framework for an authentic response to the limitations and frustrations of human existence. Nevertheless, any kind of ontology remains incomplete unless it is rooted in the daily experience of a particular people.

This book examines the reality and potential of life within the context of contemporary Africa. Given the clouded nature of the human quest for meaning, how are we to live authentic lives in the face of untold suffering and apparent social nihilism within the continent of Africa? And given the prevailing hermeneutics of ambivalence, can any meaning be found in a history in which Africans are *forever* the underdogs? How are Africans, and others with a concern for Africa, to escape a sense of estrangement in the 21st century? These are some of the questions with which we will wrestle in the ensuing chapters.

For the African people, the philosophy of being cannot be considered without recourse to a moral universe in which the ancestral spirits reign as custodians of the moral order of things. Ancestors are the guarantors of the tradition, which in turn supplies the moral code of the culture and indicates what people must do to live ethically. Ultimately, for Africans the basis of moral life is God. In a study of African moral traditions, Laurenti Magesa observes that any thought, word or act is generally understood in terms of good and evil, in the sense that such an attitude or behaviour either enhances or diminishes life.

Morality, like life, is predicated on a web of relationships. The human condition is such that we make enquiries about the nature and meaning of being. Being is discovered beyond oneself, so meaning is always to be found in encounter with the "other". Human beings achieve wholeness of meaning only in relation to that ultimate reality present within the ultimate concerns of the community. Even so, we may encounter ultimate reality in what we see, touch and feel – and yet remain unable to fathom what we have encountered because our eyes are weak and our senses numb. Accordingly, questions arising out of human experience find expression in anxiety. How is this situation to be transformed into one of hope?

According to Tillich, our ultimate concern is that which determines our state of being or non-being. From beyond ourselves, God extends the possibility to transform the content of our shattered hope through the new being in Christ. Thus, in Tillich's imagery, tomorrow becomes not merely the child of yesterday but a newborn brought forth both in gratefulness for the past and also in renewed, hopeful anticipation of the promised future.

The courage to be and the courage to hope

While inspired by Tillich's famous title, *The Courage to Be*, I believe that in Africa today hope is the appropriate outcome of human courage. For Tillich, the concept of courage had two sides: ontological and ethical. In *The Courage to Hope*, I am suggesting that by daring to hope the African people will affirm themselves, their life and their community in spite of the strong odds, anxieties and conditions which mitigate against this essential self-affirmation.

For the purpose of this book, the meaning of courage is derived from the French word *coeur*, or "heart" – the intention being to inspire Africans to hold strength of heart as a special virtue while we deal with our current predicament. Still, the courage to hope also involves Tillich's understanding of courage as "strength of mind, capable of conquering whoever (and whatever) threatens the attainment of the highest good".

Thomas Aquinas, too, delineated a theological doctrine touching on courage. In his thought, there are four cardinal virtues from the Christian perspective: wisdom, temperance, justice and courage. I have borrowed key dynamics of these four virtues in developing the theme of *The Courage to Hope*.

The goal of this book is to motivate Africans to be open to the future. The Brazilian theologian Rubem Alves has observed that, when one fears the future, "one acts in order to prevent the future from happening". This is what occurs in the political arena when sections of society resort to violence due to anxiety over the possibility of change in national leadership. Very often political violence accompanies the processes leading up to an election when the future is uncertain. How can we turn this expression of fear into hope? If it is possible to summon sufficient energy and courage, a change in mentality may result. If tomorrow is seen to bear seeds of hope, then people may act to transform the future.

The paralysis that characterizes many a political situation may be overcome through the courage to hope. When people act out of hope, they become forward-looking: they are liberated from captivity to the past and fear of a tomorrow that is no better than yesterday. They acquire positive attitudes that free them from reliance on the past as a place of retreat.

The transformation of tribalism

The courage to hope makes it possible for Africans to transcend the tribalism that has enchained the mentality of many. The courage to hope challenges Africans to venture beyond their tribal boundaries towards the wide horizons and open spaces where the rest of the human family may be encountered and appreciated. The concepts of security, tribal identity and national boundaries acquire new meaning through human interaction and unrestricted exchange of ideas. The more people interact with others outside tribal confines, the more they will learn to appreciate the commonality of their aspirations and social interests. "Otherness" ceases to represent the unknown, to be feared and resisted, and becomes instead a gateway to new opportunity and unimagined beauty.

It is generally believed that ethnic conflicts in Africa are fuelled by fierce competition for meagre resources. Here is a summary of the argument: The smaller the national cake, the more bitter the rivalry between the tribes who wish to lay some claim to a portion of that cake; access to whoever controls national resources becomes a critical factor in support for national leaders. But electing one's own to a position of power without increasing the size of the national cake will never solve the problem of poverty or heal wounds in the body politic. Therefore, generating greater wealth becomes an economic imperative in post-colonial Africa. For this reason, economic emancipation in the 21st century takes the place that was occupied in the 20th century by political self-determination.

Economic emancipation must be accompanied by spiritual emancipation. The human condition as it is now experienced in Africa is a matter of more than merely material deprivation. We must not repeat the mistake made at the time of independence by those who considered political emancipation as an end in itself.

African culture has traditionally placed a strong accent on the spiritual and ethical dimension of governance. The integrity of a leader matters more to the people than material prosperity. But this aspect of the African personality, which was central to the pan-Africanist vision of an African-led society, was lost in the rush to benefit from the spoils of colonialism. Negotiations at independence concentrated on the mechanical side of governance. The Lancaster conferences and their counterparts in French-speaking Africa focused primarily on constitutional arrangements, neglecting the ethos and ethics of government. Even the noble idea of nation-building failed to provide space for discernment of the soul of the society. Our present challenge is to incorporate such concerns in the second phase of implementing the pan-Africanist vision for the industrial and spiritual emancipation of the continent.

The courage to hope means that we shall refuse to accept our current experience of the human condition as permanent. We must negate the negation imposed by history that has created our status quo. Africans must be convinced that, despite all socio-historical factors, a better, brighter and more beautiful future is possible. We must convert our vision, aspirations and insights into a programme, just as an older generation did with regard to ending colonialism. We must defeat the Afro-pessimism that strangles nascent initiatives for transforming our present situation.

Realizing our potential

God wills that Africans live more abundant lives, but it is Africans who will determine whether that possibility is realized. God gives people the spirit and energy to embrace and nurture hope. Too frequently, hope is frustrated or wasted.

The African people, and particularly the elders, are constantly struggling to overcome forces and behaviours that diminish life and hope. Numerous symbols, sayings, parables, proverbs and rituals are employed to bring about healing and wholeness. These elements of our African heritage must be recovered, conserved and cherished. The comprehensive ethical web which runs throughout our African consciousness is a system that unites existence and action, being and doing. You are what you do – and you do what you do because of who you are.

The people of Africa understand that humanity is called to ethical discernment and action in the world. The fragile health of the continent is of grave concern, but this concern extends to the whole of creation. The ancestors teach us that we must listen to the earth, feel its pulse, if we are to recognize our connection to the sacred. Nature itself – sun, moon and stars; trees and bushes; animals and insects – manifests the glory of the Creator and links the human with the divine. The sacred character of the earth and the inter-relatedness of all things is central to the African perception of life.

Community is the place where one learns a profound respect for life. In sharing space with others, one shares one's life and experiences. A people's aspirations come to be embedded within a framework of economies of affection. While this is possible within traditional communities, the same is not true within the context of transnational corporations characterized by the economic policies, hierarchy and exclusivity of global capitalism. For this reason, the ecumenical movement has refused to compromise its commitment to a holistic, human-centred approach to development through support for sustainable communities and respect for the poor.

In African religious thought, all human beings possess an equal claim to the earth and its resources. This is especially true of the essentials that sustain life. Because they are considered sacred, these resources are thought to be owned communally. The privatization of God's generous gifts, alienating them from the whole people, is the leading cause of misery and poverty in the world today. Private ownership is a form of greed and stands in opposition to hospitality. The elders see hospitality as much as a religious and ethical duty as a civic obligation. In the generous sharing of resources, one remembers and honours the Creator for all the gifts that contribute to abundant life. Hospitality in its deepest sense negates all aspects of greed. A generation that abdicates this cardinal responsibility is guilty of great sin against humanity, the ancestors and the Creator.

The single most important criterion by which leaders are to be judged is the extent to which they contribute to the enhancement of life. They are accountable to the people and to the ancestors. Systems of law and justice should be ordered for the benefit of all elements in the community, not to serve and protect the narrow interests and property of the rich and powerful. In the African tradition, leadership ought to be changed if its practices result in the diminishing or destruction of life. The spirit of good leadership also leads inevitably to caring and compassion towards young people, especially the children.

There are many young people in Africa who desire to be safe. They seek assurance of a future that is worth the cost of enduring. They wish to participate in the creativity and innovation that will lead to a better future for their continent. The young are yearning for a new ethic that will help them build new communities founded on love. In this age of economic globalization, when society is threatened by unbridled accumulation of wealth and cut-throat competition for diminishing resources, young people are asking hard questions. But where are youth to find the social space for raising questions, and testing answers to them, in a scene dominated by the global market? How are young people to avoid addiction to market stimuli and social nihilism? What alternative ideology and structure can be offered to provide them some other option than the mistaken ideas and ideals that are so pervasive?

It is the hope of the ecumenical movement that the young people of Africa, and the rest of the world, will find within the mothering spirit of God the profound intimacy and joy to sustain a new revolution of love. The Holy Spirit, whose power brings life out of death and decay, may be trusted to lead the children of Africa to respond creatively to the ambiguities of our times. The young will seek and find Jesus in the poor and perplexed, among those who have been jailed unjustly, in the hungry and sick, and among those who have been rejected by society.

Throughout history, Africa has been faced with the fact of finitude, and with anxiety at the prospect of being engulfed by non-being. Yet we have resolved not to let go of the hand of God. If we have the courage and tenacity of our forebears, who stood firm against the injustices of slavery and colonial oppression, we shall find a way to do in our time what they did in theirs. We shall be awakened, sometime soon, to the dawning of a new day. In this time of testing, the proof of our resilience will be demonstrated in the courage to hope!

2. The Home of Humanity

Recent research in molecular biology on a genetic factor known as mitochondrial DNA appears to confirm that fully sapient man (human being) first emerged in Africa, and proposes a date somewhere between 200,000 and 100,000 years ago. It also profers the stupendous claim that the transformation from earlier forms of man was due, not to a process of parallel evolution taking place in many different parts of the Old Worlds, but rather to a fresh wave of colonization, emanating from an African base and spreading over the whole of the occupied globe, with a minimum of hybridization with earlier strains of man.

Roland Oliver, *The African Experience*

Africa is the primordial home of all humanity. Recent scientific and historical findings have confirmed beyond speculation the African origin of human existence. Not only is Africa the primordial garden but it is also the sacred custodian of the most ancient civilizations that existed and gave birth to the classical and modern worlds. Africa nourished a diversity of traditions, values and spirituality that has come to constitute the fabric of human culture. The garden grandeur of Eden, long buried beyond the realm of history, is recalled in the heart of Africa through an unavoidable consciousness of the abundance of life.

Life brings life into being. The universe, the sky, the ocean, the forest, hills, mountains, animals, the spirit – all came to be, because life spoke. Life expresses itself through life. Eden is said to have been imbued with the cosmic ingredients that sustain life in all its forms upon earth. It is the true home of all species. The biblical tradition of the Garden of Eden is a basic resource for an integrated understanding of the origin, meaning and ecology of human and all other life-forms in the universe. The utopian myth of Eden provides the stimulus for a holistic vision of life. The fullness of life shared by all created things is experienced in the harmony of their interdependence and in their common dependence on God, the ground of being. Eden becomes an ethical symbol for renewed enthusiasm in life. The garden comes to symbolize a life in which all is interwoven until the many textures, though different, seem to blend as one. That garden is Africa.

The primordial garden

In his *Introduction to African Civilizations*, John Jackson traces the origins of humanity and civilization to Ethiopia and Egypt. He also describes the racist bias of many Western historians who have attempted to erase the influence of Africa from the historical record. It is essential that we recover the significance of African heritage for human origins and for the subsequent development of the whole world.

If the narrative legends concerning the Garden of Eden described a location within the modern borders of Iran or Iraq, the scientific-historical locus of the primordial garden in which humans first drew breath is somewhere in Africa. It is to be found where the anthills of the savanna are scattered among equatorial forests and mountains on either side of the Great Rift Valley as it runs south from the ancient city of Axum towards the Cape of Good Hope. For 200,000 years, this was humanity's only home.

Roland Oliver has described Africa as a vibrant symbol, the *ecofilia*, a living mandala representing the affinity of life forms existing in harmony with the human spirit. Thus, Africa as our common cradle invites all humanity to participate in a spirituality and reverence for the earth that combine in a sacrament of life. The rich diversity of all the species inhabiting this world manifests the benevolence of their Creator.

But the Garden of Eden is known to be a place that offers radical choices which may define our destiny. In the midst of the garden stands the tree of the knowledge of good and evil. Eating its fruit introduces us into a drama of uncertainties and poses the grave dangers to be found in disobedience and disharmony. The garden is the stage on which the drama is set that not only defines but also may defy human destiny. Here is the arena of conflict between the forces of good and evil. At the same time, the earth preserves harmony of spirit with the common ground of being. In the rich earth and its potential, we encounter both the muse of life and the source of human destiny.

Air, water, soil, rock, fire and wind are sacramental elements of our mother universe, speaking to one another in the same language and interwoven by the invincible will of life. The planet earth is the sanctuary of life in the universe. Often lost in the discourse of history, the narrative of the Garden of Eden preserves a vision of an eco-utopia manifested in time and space. Is this ancient vision now to be replaced by "history"? If so, whose version of history are we to trust? Is the vision of eco-utopia to be explained away as a folk-tale about a place that humans were thought to have shared with a mythical god in some distant, tribal past? Or does this story continue to carry existential meaning as we seek to define sacred ground, the experience of intrinsic immanence and the open market-place of life that we call "the world"?

The imaging of Africa

This noble planet, full of life, continues on its voyage of creation. New life is brought forth. Life is nurtured through the cycles of nature. The twofold motion of the blue planet creates time for the intervention of history and space to sustain the resources of the earth. The light that shines upon earth is a greening light, revealing all the contents of earth-bound reality and showing the extent of human choice.

Africa, the garden of our common beginnings, resounds to echoes of Eden, the true home of the human spirit. Amid the lush bounty of Africa, it is possible to imagine that eco-utopia where creation in its full integrity communes with a fulfilled humanity upon the sacred ground of being. Yet, while the mythical garden was established as a place for obedience to the laws of nature and selection of good over evil, the living continent of Africa has become the crucible of history, a place of struggle to regain human dignity, integrity and freedom to make choices affecting the future.

Creation in Africa is understood in terms of the household of life in which relationships take precedence over struggles for consumption or domination. The household of life is not only characteristic but is also singular evidence of the greatest possible act of benevolence. The garden is a testing ground of faithfulness which stems out of the responsibility to care for the earth, a responsibility entrusted to humankind. The myth of the garden does not contain ingredients of historicity for empirical analysis; rather, it is a foundational metaphor rich in the sense of a tremendous opportunity lost by humankind. The story informs us that man and woman are not endowed with clarity of vision, due either to utter carelessness on their part or their blind pursuit of wealth, power and prestige. The tragedy that alienates humankind from the primordial garden, the eco-utopia, is our refusal to live in harmony with the cosmos and, therefore, to form an affinity with the common ground of being. The integrity of all creation is shown as the lost nexus of the divine and the human spirit.

Let us consider the gift of life that the human species fully realized in Africa. It is not my intention here to delve into details of recent findings in palaeontology, but to raise some critical theological implications based on those findings and how they may impact on the global perception and understanding of Africa. The question of Africa's calling as the mother of all humanity has always been subject to controversy and to deliberate falsifications of history. Not even African theologians and philosophers have paid enough attention to Africa's role as mother of humanity. Contemporary research into the historical origins of the human species has yet to gain theological currency, or to receive much attention in any standard treatment of the continent.

The predominant tendency in the modern imaging of Africa does not reflect her unparalleled place as mother of all. Despite the hardships and suffering of her people as a result of centuries of genocide and enslavement by prodigal civilizations, she continues to be humiliated by contemporary historical events and ideological trends that persist in undermining broad appreciation of her heritage.

The ancestral heritage

Despite many obstacles, grandeur and goodness within creation still are experienced in the vast terrain of the African landscape. Genetic self-sufficiency of the human race was guaranteed by prehistoric events and encounters on this continent. The first exodus out of Africa may have happened 50,000 years ago. Before that, the collectives and communities of this ancient world schooled humans to be what they are today. Humans, having found their first home on planet earth, began their pilgrimage to civilization by first adapting basic survival skills and communal systems that preserved the values of equanimity.

The Catholic anthropologist and theologian Teilhard de Chardin penned a memorable passage about how silently the human person had made entry upon the scene of world history: "He trod so softly that when his presence was at last betrayed by the indestructible evidence of his stone tools... he was already spread across the ancient world from the Cape of Good Hope to Peking." That was how it looked before radiometric dating made it possible to compare the chronology of sites in Europe, Asia and Africa. It was written before excavations around Lake Turkana had shown that, in eastern Africa at least, it is just possible to identify hominid remains that antedate the earliest stone artefacts.

A consciousness that Africa was the original home of humanity preceded the conclusions of modern science. It began with the project of racial liberation in plantation societies in the Caribbean islands established as colonies of European imperialism between the 16th and 19th centuries. On the African continent, the political elite who had just returned sated with the elixirs of Western education and encounters with the black world in diaspora became the object of hope for self-determination. The Caribbean experience was unique in the sense that it went beyond the racial historicism of Marcus Garvey and embraced the intertwined dimensions of class and racial factors in the works of such authors as Frantz Fanon and Walter Rodney. Beyond cultural excavation, it was the Senegalese scholar Chiek Anta Diop who began to explore in profound depth the place of Egypt in the quest for a renewed vision of Africa as home of all humanity. His works became part of the International Scientific Committee of UNESCO's *General History of Africa*. It has now been convincingly demonstrated that the ancient Egyptians were of African descent and that their ancestors did not, as once argued, migrate from the Ancient Near East. The Greek culture that is considered to be the cradle of Western civilization owes her rational systems to the traditions of sapience of the Egyptian world. The great irony is that Herodotus, the Greek "father of history", attributes the science, religion and philosophy for which the Greeks are praised as having been acquired from Egypt.

At that time, Egypt accounted for more than half the population of the African continent. Beyond Egypt, in sub-Saharan Africa, centres of learning stretched from Timbuktu to the kingdom of Axum to the glories reflected in the modern ruins of Zimbabwe, and back again past the fabled Benin Bronzes to the majesty of Carthage. Axum, an ancient, almost mythical, city-state, existed about 2500 years ago and was situated in the far northern plateau of modern-day Ethiopia. The people of Axum, with Sudan, dominated the ivory market through trade routes that stretched all the way to Timbuktu, the Mediterranean region and parts of the Near East. In those ancient times on the continent of Africa, there were already in place the production of coins as a medium of exchange, and a steady migration of Greco-Roman merchants landing at the port of Adulis and elsewhere. Today, massive ruins reveal the amazing civilization of this great kingdom south of Egypt. The discovery of the great walls of Zimbawe, in modern Zimbabwe, further illustrates that the African "hinterland" excelled in architectural technology and that Egypt was not necessarily the epitome of Africa's contribution to world civilization.

Not all African peoples founded states. The hunters and gatherers did not do so, for their communities were too small and spread too thinly to require such organization. The nomadic and other pastoral tribes did not normally form states, although they sometimes took over by conquest the states of others. Among cultivators, the inhabitants of mountainous areas, living on ridges and divided from each other by steep valleys, often felt no need for communities wider than those of kinship. Sometimes, as in Morocco, such areas were actually enclosed within the frontiers of a large state, yet no attempt was made to conquer and govern them.

Nevertheless, most Africans did live in states, apparently from quite early in the Iron Age, and these were invariably in some sense hereditary monarchies. The tradition of primogeniture was rare. Usually, systems of succession provided a choice of candidates from among a limited group of "royals". Sometimes this choice could be managed peacefully by a group of inner counsellors, but often it would be decided by warlike means. In Ganda, the dominant language of the Ugandan region, the word for a "reign" is *mirembe*, which originally meant the period of peace following a succession struggle – expected to last for years rather than for weeks or months.

African perspectives on creation

African origin narratives take a primarily symbolic or hierophanic approach to everyday reality. Objects such as earth, sun, moon or stars, as well as such social practices as marriage, sacrifice or agricultural production, and developmental processes such as health, illness or the building of identity are seen more in light of their capacity to be symbols of the spiritual than in everyday terms. This approach subordinated the economic, political, cultural and biological dimensions of everyday life to the spiritual domain. This ordering is the opposite of the modern arrangement that sees the spiritual world subjected to other considerations, or eliminates it altogether. These narratives of the origin of life in the universe are not so much magical as filled with moral and existential content. Nor are they an attempt to prove the nature of existence in empirical terms. Their mythic-poetic content assumes a system of beliefs regarding causality and synchronicity that conflict with many Western and modern assumptions.

In African tradition, the spiritual world is simply accepted as a matter of fact since it precedes and contains the very matrix of human experience. The void, symbolizing a state of non-space and absence of matter, was transformed by the wind blowing as creative spirit whose power over dark matter no one may fathom. In the absolute silence of chaos, something happened that would lead to life in the universe as we know it today.

Most ancient civilizations in the Far East, especially the Chinese and Hindu dynastic systems, conceived history as consisting of cosmic cycles. The cyclical nature of time in the Oriental world is not merely a mythical means of comprehending the enigma and paradox of creation. It is a Promethean vision of reality that encompasses a philosophical world-view. In fact, many contemporary, scientific theories of cosmology feature a pulsating model of the universe. Could it be that Friedmann's theory of cosmic oscillation is the scientific counterpart of the ancient Eastern idea of the eternal return, or that the multi-billion-year duration from "big bang" to "big crunch" might represent the "great year" of the life-cycle of Brahma?

On the other hand, there are modern scientific initiatives like the "steady-state theory" of cosmology that claim an endless process of creation without the possibility of external intervention. According to this innovation, even the big bang would no longer be plausible because there is no need for any kind of supernatural explanation for the origin and nature of the universe. According to such a theory, any vision of the cosmos based on the notion of eternal recurrence or presence could not, strictly speaking, accommodate the idea of a personal, self-existent being as creator. Such systems are essentially polytheistic or non-theistic.

What do we find in exploring the African terrain? Africans see themselves as inhabitants of a moral universe surrounded by a community of cosmic and sentient beings bound together by the vital force of life. Life is not recycled unendingly but recedes to the frontier of the spirits at death, where it is preserved as part of the cosmos within the realm of moral agents. The cosmos itself which is the home of all sentient and spiritual beings had its origin in time, but whether or not it may have pre-existed in other forms is not known. What is perceived by many African cultures is that the Most Gracious One, the mother of all that we see, after creating the universe went far away beyond the realm of the spirits and related to the cosmos only through her moral agents, namely the ancestral spirits. They remained links and emissaries to the human community and custodians of the vital force of life. This African world-view is primarily derived from the moral tradition of abundant life. For this reason, the notion of a moral universe is nurtured by a profound affection for the integrity, the inter-relatedness, of life.

To cite an example of the teaching in just one culture, the Luo people who live in the fertile region near the source of the Nile teach that the moral responsibility of the human community is the preservation and transmission of the vital force of life. This responsibility is at the heart of the survival and continuity of life from one generation to another. It is a responsibility bequeathed upon all human beings by *Murungu*, God, and overseen by the great ancestors. The vital force is an invincible, self-generating power in the universe that creates and renews life in all sentient beings. This force resides in all human beings and is brought to fruition in birth, sustained and nurtured in the rich network of communal relationships, and transferred back to the community in the spiritual realm through death. Even after people die, they are thought to remain part of the web of cosmic relationships that sustain life in the universe. People are not recycled at death, nor do they recede to some invisible frontier of the spirit. When humans die, they continue within the cosmos as moral agents of the vital force. In other words, with the passage of time, and specifically through the occasion of death, one is initiated into the community of ancestral spirits.

But what is the nature of this vital force, how does it function and within which medium is it transmitted? It is not a cognitive force because its impulse does not appear exclusively within the realm of causality. Yet it is transmitted effectively within the domain of the physical universe. Life comes where nothing had been, and everything is constantly being sublimated into something beyond the reach of time. No form of human knowledge can explain adequately the ultimate meaning underlying the origin of things.

For Africans, the deepest foundation of the existence of all things is found not in nothing but in God. However, we derive functional meaning from relationships between things in the universe. This outlook is shared widely by most Nilotic and Bantu tribes and is primarily derived from an existential vision of life, a vision that finds expression in rituals celebrating the events of life and death.

In naming ceremonies, new life is venerated as a miracle. The rituals performed in the event of death provide a safe passage of initiation to the life hereafter. The sages, mediums or tribal leaders facilitate this safe passage on behalf of the community. No one has the authority to change or eliminate the details of ritual observance. The community is uneasy about change in ritual based not just on the fate of the individual in question but also out of concern for siblings and the general welfare of those who were closely related to the dead. It is a bad omen for the whole clan if one of their prominent members is not accorded a decent burial. This could haunt and torment the whole community for generations to come until cleansing rituals involving the family of the deceased are instituted for their sake and that of the community.

Thus, the moral universe is nurtured not only through the relational value of all life within the cosmos but especially by the network of human relationships that define moments of transition to new life. Such are the moments of birth and death in which life comes as a blessing to the community and filters into the unknown realm where the spirits abide. These are transcendent moments and no one, however educated or cultured, questions the norms by which they are preserved. Only the ancestors in their wisdom take precedence over such matters, and human beings are held accountable by the manner in which they conduct themselves with regard to ritual observance.

Outside the rituals, there are customs and beliefs which determine human behaviour during defining moments of life and death. The values and general conduct of the African people based on their cosmology are in turn sustained by a profound affection for the integrity of life. Moral cosmology in African traditions is also predicated on the belief that all humans are moral beings, conscious of the difference between good and evil, with a felt obligation to pursue the former and avoid the latter. This serves as yet another way of describing ourselves as incurably "moral" creatures. If we were non-moral creatures, like plants and ants, we would lack any sense of the morally good as distinct from the morally evil. The human condition is at the heart of this universe which is held together not by dualistic systems or the eternal wheel of time but by institutions of affection. In other words, Africans long have held a moral cosmology in which both the cyclical concept of the wheel of time and the linear concept of the arrow of time are entirely subordinate to the intrinsically relational web of life. Greek philosophy, which is the foundation of Western dualism, long remained obsessed with the concept of eternal cosmic cycles. This idea of the cyclical nature of time was later inherited by the Arabs, who embraced Greek culture, until it finally resurfaced in medieval Christendom thanks to the scholastic preference for Aristotelian modes of argument.

The Bible and history

The linear historical perspective often ascribed to the Christian Bible has a certain appeal within African cultures, yet there is also a recognition that a purely linear approach is an oversimplification of the intricate web of life. The linear world-view is derived from a profound sense that the universe had a definite origin in time followed by specific periods of divine interventions and struggles with humanity that ultimately will determine its final destiny somewhere in the future. It is characterized by the belief that God created the universe "in the beginning", that is, at a specific time in the past, and subsequently God has been in dialogue with humankind through cosmic events and personal encounters. Christians go so far as to believe that, at a specific moment in history, the divine has entered into the realm of historical time and shared the human condition. The final book of the Christian Bible, Revelation, provides a vision of the End towards which God is shepherding humanity.

At the centre of this view of creation is the conviction that the creator is entirely separate from and independent of creation itself, and yet always is engaged with it. Thus, the universe is in no way an extension of God's self-existent being. This brings into question the whole discussion of whether God exists outside the realm of historical time, the notion of God as eternal and thus removed from time and space. God may be everlasting, but God is also everlastingly engaged in history.

That God is everlasting assumes a being whose presence not only transcends but is also interwoven with history, a being who is omnipresent. Nothing whatsoever exists beyond God's knowledge, not even the human ego. Here the idea of individuality needs to be revisited in relation to African cosmology. For example, among the Akan people of Ghana, there are at least three basic parts to the human person: the *okra*, or soul; the *sunsum*, or ego; and the *honan*, or body. The individual is "the ontic unity" of these three parts. The *okra* is the divine spark of *Onyame*, the creator God who exists in all human beings. Often, this presence escapes the awareness of the ordinary individual who is conscious only of the *sunsum* and *honan*. In its subconscious depths, the *okra* carries *Onyame*'s plans for each individual, so that its relation to the *sunsum* is predestinarian. The *okra*'s impact is experienced as having a determinative power that cannot be ignored with impunity by the *sunsum*. Not surprisingly, spiritual beings, whether deities or ancestors, have often been seen as ambivalent authority figures with the power to intervene constructively or destructively in the human process of self-formation. They had the power to steer and redirect human life in spite of the narrower concerns of the *sunsum*. This guidance had as its aim making humans more aware of the cosmic order of which they were a part, and with which they must seek harmony. Wherever there is a creature, the inescapable creator God is present and relates to the creature in a personal and experiential mode.

The source of life

But traditions and theologians within Christianity have disagreed over the eternal God's relationship to the world of history. In the story of creation as found in the book of Genesis, we encounter a paradox. While God seems to act within the realm of time, it is equally true that God somehow exists outside time! If God is eternal, and time is part of the physical universe – i.e., part of creation, as St Augustine claimed – then certainly God must be outside time. It must be possible to speak of God apart from history.

Today, the nearest we have come to a commonly accepted scientific explanation of the origin of the universe is the big-bang theory which postulates that the entire universe came into being about fifteen billion years ago with a magnificent explosion. At that very moment, says the theory, space was infinitely shrunk, and since there would be no time without space, even time was non-existent. Thus, material singularity is also space-time singularity. Because all laws of physics are formulated in terms of space and time, these laws cannot apply beyond the point at which space and time cease to exist. Hence, the laws of physics break down at the singularity of the big bang. In other words, we cannot know when the big bang occurred since it did not happen within the realm of time and space. We cannot even refer to what preceded the big bang as "before".

Returning to African cosmology, let us imagine that the deep void symbolized a state of non-space timelessness and absence of matter. And imagine that the wind was the creative spirit of God whose power over dark matter no one can fathom. In absolute darkness and silence, something happened which in billions of years would lead to life in the universe as we know it today. And so, with Augustine, one may hold by reasonable faith that whatever it is that happened, it could not have happened within the realm of historical time; neither does this event seem to belong to the classic philosophical categories of causation.

Nothing created, not even the deep void itself, preceded the divine spirit. The origin of all things lies in the goodness of God. The idea that all things came into existence out of nothing – in Western thought called "creation *ex nihilo*" – flies in the face of the so-called pagan mythologies of creation that allude to the existence of some primordial stuff on which deities were dependent in creating the universe. Even the Platonic notion of creation depicted a demi-urge replicating into the sensible world poor copies of ideas from the realm of forms. For Plato, the world and everything in it was but a shadow of reality. The true embodiment of reality was the soul which longed to contemplate the eternal, immutable truths in the world of forms. The demi-urge was restricted by having to work with pre-existing, and imperfect, material.

It is clear in Genesis that the biblical creator is not subordinate to anything, not even time or space, whether before, during or after the creation of the universe. God calls everything into existence out of love and recognizes its goodness. Each element of creation is declared good in a sequence described with poetic joy – until, at last, humanity is portrayed living in a blissful garden as steward of the created world.

For Africans, it is essential to remember that creation is an act unique to God. Life does not spring from nothing but from the goodness of God. Arguments over creation *ex nihilo* are irrelevant to a fundamental tenet of African thought, in the sense that they are based on the idea of physical causality while in African theology it is moral causality that precedes every act of creation. In the cosmogonic myths of Africa, the temporality of divine projects does not follow a purely linear path. Time "lasts" as long as the deities continue the work of creation. These projects may be seen to follow a cyclical path that encompasses material birth from the spiritual world, death, return to the spiritual world and rebirth. This eternal cycle defines the cosmological conception of time in traditional African philosophy. Like time, space is related to the continuing project of creation. Among the Akan, for example, *Onyame* is the creator of space and time, yet at the same time he is beyond both. He is boundless and "cannot be limited to any particular region of space" or to any period of time. Time and space are thus categories that help to frame the project of creation, but they do not in any way limit or constrain the creator.

African cosmology tells of a moral universe in which the human community is responsible for preservation and transmission of the vital force of life. This responsibility is at the heart of survival and continuity of life from one generation to the next. It is a responsibility bequeathed upon humans by God and overseen by the ancestors. The image of creative divinity, analogous to the creative individual, becomes crucial for the cosmogonic framing of African ontology; that is to say, it is essential to our interpretation of the meaning of existence. Within this framework, our existence is seen to be the result of creative work by deities and ancestors. It is their creative project – to make, regulate and unmake. Beyond that, God as ultimate creator is the absolute reality: *Onyame*, transcending human perceptions of personhood, is revealed to be Alone, Boundless, Architect, Originator, Omniscient, Omnipotent, Uncreated and Eternal. God – in Soyinka's phrase, the "vortex of archetypes" – is the origin of all that exists, the absolute ground of being, the sole and whole explanation of the universe, the source of life.

3. The Dilemma and Dreams of Pan-Africanism

Human civilization was Western in the eyes of the colonizers, and Africans were, at least for Tempels in the 1930s, not quite human. What they were, whether pure children or incipient human beings in need of tutoring, was simply the result of the application of Western standards within a non-Western context.

V.Y.Mudimbe, *The Invention of Africa,* p.68

In this chapter, we shall navigate the historical landscape of the dreams and dilemmas of pan-Africanism. Recounting events in the great story of the African survival of the tragedies is vital, even when it may seem repetitive. It is the cleansing of memories and regaining of right perspectives on events as they truly happened. Africa is on a journey of historical dilemmas. Because the journey is real, the future is also one of real hope. Yet, in a journey, one is always confronted by the dilemma of the ever-changing conditions of life and human history. For example, in his autobiography, Malcolm X narrated his political journey from slavery to freedom and also described his religious quest, the journey of self-realization as felt and experienced in spiritual terms.

We are a species puzzled by movement and hence puzzled by change. The dialectic of being and non-being has often led to a synthesis of nothingness, a seeming impasse at the precipice of nihilism and despair. Long gone is the clarity of the biblical invocation of light from darkness on a first day and recurring days of division into neat divides of land and sky, earth and heaven, low and high. Lines drawn in the sand are, in the final analysis, lines that can be washed away.

One cannot of course do justice to the whole spectrum of information on pan-Africanism in one chapter. Nevertheless, it would be imprudent to engage in a discourse of hope for the continent without tracing the various paths that eventually led to legal freedom and self-rule. It represents a short span of history, and we are still in the midst of it. The future is still cooking inside the pots of transition. Hence, however hobbled the moment may be, or unpromising the times may seem, there is still something to work towards and hope for in Africa. We shall begin with the story of slavery and the birth of pan-Africanism.

The slave trade

The experience of slavery and slave trade is one of history's greatest manifestations of human misery. Apart from the Holocaust, it is the most disturbing form of genocidal cruelty and hatred inflicted with impunity upon a section of the human race. There are many disturbing questions which remain unanswered; in fact, even public acknowledgment of the crimes against humanity has been extremely hard to come by in our time. The silence of modern European nations on the question of reparations deepens the historical dilemma of how Africa should relate to Europe and the rest of the world. Even if Africa were to forgive, who would receive or accept that forgiveness without someone acknowledging publicly the burden of guilt?

From an ethical point of view, slavery sought to destroy the very fabric of being that constitutes what is human. Slavery in all its forms is designed to humiliate unto death the human self and instead replace it with a mundane form of servitude which not only undermines the dignity of the person but also defiles the image of God in human relations. The Euro-American slave trade was based on a specific ideological construction of the other and a particular anthropology based on racism. Racial construction of otherness ensures that one particular race will have the grip of power and control of all resources and access to the wealth of this world. The amazing cruelty and humiliation inflicted upon Africans as late as the 1900s is unparalleled in the history of crimes against humanity.

The very fabric of the human identity and being of the African people was put on trial and executed during and after the slave trade. It is a miracle that people of African descent survived the genocide, but the slow social suicide lingers on in memories of struggle and despair. In the gospel according to William Lynch, a Caribbean slave-owner of the 1700s, the principles of slave ownership were as follows:

Both the horse and the nigger are no good to the economy in the wild or natural state. Both must be broken and tied together for orderly production. For an orderly future, special and particular attention must be paid to the female and the young offspring. Both must be crossbred to produce a variety and division of labour.

Both must be taught to respond to a peculiar new language. Psychological and physical instruction of containment must be created for both. In other words break the will to resist. Now the breaking process is the same for both the horse and the nigger – only slightly varying in degree. But as we said before, there is an art in long-range economic planning. You must keep your eye and thoughts on the offspring of the horse and nigger... for example, take the case of the wild stud horse, a female horse and an already infant horse; and compare the breaking process with two captured nigger males in their natural state, a pregnant nigger woman with their infant offspring... when it comes to breaking the uncivilized nigger, take the meanest and most restless nigger, strip him of his clothes in front of the remaining male, the female, and the nigger infant; tar and feather him, tie each leg to a different horse faced in opposite directions, set him afire and beat both horses to pull him apart in front of the remaining nigger. The next step is to take a bullwhip and beat the remaining nigger male to the point of death in front of the female and the infant. Don't kill him, but put the fear of God into him.

Quoted in *New African,* no. 398, pp.30-31

Slavery and slave trade was a systematic, well thought-out and carefully designed economic project whose philosophy of white supremacy raises deep ethical and existential questions of race relations. The use of human and animal labour with impunity as equal factors in satisfying the desires of the slave master is incomprehensible unless there is a deep confluence of need in agricultural production and the evil of racism itself. The church is yet to be absolved of its role in the enslavement of other races. Historians like John Jackson argue that the very idea of using Africans as slaves in the Americas was initiated by a Catholic bishop.

Following the Spanish conquest of Mexico and Peru, the natives of these lands were forced into slave labour in the mines. But owing to their high death rate, it became necessary for the European masters to seek alternative labour.

Bartolomé de las Casas, bishop of Chiapa, in 1517 came to their rescue by proposing that each Spanish gentleman be permitted to import twelve African slaves. Jackson relates that this advice was adopted by the king of Spain, who issued a patent to one of his friends giving him the authority to import four thousand black slaves annually to Cuba, Hispaniola, Jamaica and Puerto Rico.

Henceforth, the traffic of human cargo from Africa to the Americas increased in volume and eventually became uncontrollable with nearly all European nations participating in the slave trade. As we have already pointed out, by the 1700s the enslavement reached its most inhuman levels, characterized as it was by unimaginable cruelty meted out to the slaves. When such treatment became a subject of criticism by the advocates of the abolition of slavery, the European slave owners invoked the endorsement of the Christian church in an effort to ease their consciences. Chaplin Cohen delivered the most scathing indictment when he said,

> The peculiar and damning fact in the history of slavery, so far as the Christian church is concerned, is this... It was created by Christians, it was continued by Christians, it was in some respects more barbarous than anything the world had yet seen, and its worst features were to be witnessed in countries that were most ostentatious in their parade of Christianity.

> Quoted by Jackson

Given the deep involvement by church leaders and Christians in imagining and managing African enslavement, the church has a moral burden to come up with language and symbols with which to express public acknowledgment and repentance. This calls for profound remembering as a prerequisite for healing of memories and reconciliation. More than any other calamity, the European slave trade dehumanized the African people and grossly violated their dignity.

A step towards restorative justice was suggested by the late Church of South India bishop Lesslie Newbigin when he visited Elmira Castle, which was once a slave depot on the coast of Ghana. Finding that the chapel of the castle was built directly over the dungeon where the slaves were kept before being shipped off to America, and that a hole was cut in the chapel floor so that the British at prayer could keep an eye on the captured Africans, Newbigin wrote:

> I am always amazed that these crimes can be so easily forgotten. Ever since that visit I have wished that some representative Englishman – an archbishop or prime minister – might come to Ghana and go down into that dungeon, kneel down on the floor and offer a prayer of contrition. I still hope it may happen.

Geiko Müller-Fahrenholz, *The Art of Forgiveness*, p.66

A fitting tribute to Bishop Newbigin would be for the British churches to heed his wish.

There are fundamental moral questions that must be faced even after the deliberations and findings of the UN World Conference against Racism, Racial Discrimination, Xenophobia and Related Intolerance, held in Durban, South Africa, in September 2001. Contemporary discourse on race remains stigmatized by the lack of historical consciousness, denial and discomfort in facing the realities of memory.

The popular resistance of black people against slavery began with both spiritual and political movements in the diaspora. It was Haiti that became the first black nation in the world to lead resistance against slavery and colonialism. The utility of cultural resources and spirituality in language and actions is what led to the initiation of black revolution throughout the world.

Voodoo was indeed one of the few areas of spiritual autonomy and activity of the African slaves. As a religion and a vital spiritual force, it became a source of psychological liberation and the cultural fabric of self-determination. Voodoo further enabled slaves to break away from real chains of slavery and to see themselves as independent persons with the dignity worthy of human beings whose right to life and freedom is paramount.

But, in so far as voodoo remained merely a means of spiritual self-expression and of psychological or cathartic release from material subjugation, it was of little use as a tool in the struggle for liberation. It became necessary, therefore, to transform the dynamic found in voodoo into a political and moral principle affirming the consciousness of slaves as autonomous beings. Otherwise, the status quo could have been perpetuated. It was only when slaves were able to translate their consciousness into active rebellion and, finally, into the life-and-death struggle of revolution aimed at the total destruction of their masters and of slavery, that emancipation could and did become a reality. The drive to affirm one's own existence and the urge to destroy the oppressor became as fundamental a part of the slaves' daily existence as had been submissiveness and accommodation in appearance.

The rise of revolution

Significantly, revolts and conspiracies that did occur in Saint Domingue (Haiti) happened in a relatively early period of the colony's economic and socio-political development, the very first one occurring in 1622 when the island was still entirely under Spanish rule. Within the twenty-five years between 1679 and 1704, four other armed conspiracies had been planned by slaves in different parts of French Saint Domingue, all aimed at the massacre and annihilation of their white masters. In the end, they were localized affairs that the authorities quickly crushed, and so collective armed revolt remained at this time a limited form of slave resistance with minimal chances of success. Of the many and diverse forms of resistance, *marroonage* proved in the end to be the most viable and certainly the most consistent. From the beginning of the colony under Spanish rule, throughout its long history under France, until the abolition of slavery in 1793, slaves defied the system that denied them the most essential social and human right: the right to be a free person. They mobilized themselves apart from Europeans into small groups ("petit marroonage") as well as into large established communities ("gran' marroonage"), in organized armed bands or posing as free persons with a trade in the urban centres. They established themselves in the forests, raided the plantations at night, pillaging, ransacking, sometimes even devastating the plantation to secure food.

When caught, they would once again be subjected to the laws and practices governing slavery. Characteristically, it was in the voodoo ceremonies that African traditional languages, dance, religious world-view and medicine were all evident. Various African languages constituted in themselves a form of cultural protest. Slave resistance had spanned several countries and was expressed or carried out by slaves in many ways. Partial revolts, conspiracies, plots to kill the master, suicide, infanticide, voodoo, poisoning and marroonage with its long and diverse history, all bore witness to the slave's human spirit to assert an independent will.

In 1791 this consciousness became collective when, beginning in northern Haiti, entire plantations of slaves deserted in a rapid succession to join what had become a massive revolutionary army. The army was a highly disciplined and broadly based organization, and enjoyed widespread participation and popular support. Although somewhat fragmented, there is evidence to suggest that in fact a few of the early leaders of popular resistance (notably Doukman and Jean Francois) had acquired skills elsewhere. It was the French revolution that provided the opportunity for the great revolt. Thus, news of the revolution in France which sought to destroy the monarchy and the oppressive feudal system trickled down to Haiti, leading to mass protests against propertied classes. Even the disenfranchized white colonial settlers had first responded to news from France by claiming their rights and demanding abolition of the economic and commercial restrictions laid upon them by the imperial regime. Talk of liberty, equality and fraternity then fell upon the receptive ears of domestic slaves.

Saint Domingue does indeed stand out as a unique instance as it is the only place where resold slaves succeeded in abolishing slavery. Saint Domingue emerged from its revolution as a politically independent state. The ideology of the French revolution certainly had an impact upon the unfolding and development of the revolution in Saint Domingue but, even then, it did not in itself produce those events. Ultimately, if the material conditions and stage of development had not been what they were in Saint Domingue by the third quarter of the 18th century, the French revolutionary ideology may not necessarily have led to the tremendous explosion of events that occurred.

The 1791 revolt was led by slaves from the upper echelons of the slave system; among them were notable commandeers, coachmen, domestics and a few mulatto slaves. Among the free blacks was Toussaint L'Ouverture. Voodoo played an important role in welding together the slaves in the 1791 revolt in the north and in some early struggles in the west. In the south, there was no evidence of voodoo as an organizational vehicle. The commandeers played a pivotal leadership role. Generally, the slaves followed these leaders' decision or authoritative directives to rebel.

The slave leaders of the platoon movement in the south had originally demanded, as did Jean Francois and Biassou in the north, the freedom of three or four hundred of their chief officers and secondary leaders. They did not from the beginning demand the outright abolition of slavery. Though their demands were never granted, this did mark the beginning of development of the freedom struggle and consciousness in the slaves. The rebellion in the north was led and directed entirely by leaders who commanded a solid army from the outset. Under Jean Francois and Biassou, they were closely allied with counter-revolutionary French elements and with the Spanish fighting for freedom but in the name of monarchy and royalism. Thus Saint Domingue became independent in 1804 as a result of the popular slave uprising. It is with this background of a successful movement against slavery and colonialism in the diaspora that we can begin to explore the origin of the idea of pan-Africanism.

The movement towards pan-Africanism

Pan-Africanism was originally conceived by a West Indian barrister by the name of Henry Sylvester William who practised law in London at the end of 19th century. At this time, Africans were facing systematic colonization and exploitation of land by imperial powers and settlers. Many South and West African chiefs went to England to protest against this deprivation of their rights. The first pan-African conference was organized by William in London in 1900 to combat aggressive policies of the British imperialists. The idea therefore first rose as a manifestation of fraternal solidarity among Africans and peoples of African descent in diaspora. As the ideological embodiment of black struggle, pan-Africanism can be traced to the ex-slaves in the Americas and West Indies. Africans from the continent of Africa became more significantly involved in the movement at the fifth pan-Africanist congress in Manchester, England, in 1945. Finally, pan-Africanism gained roots in the soil of Africa at a conference of independent African states in 1958 at Accra in Ghana.

The first wave of pan-Africanism was dominated by the desire of the ex-slaves to come back to Africa. It was initially known as the "Back to Africa Movement". An ex-slave by the name of Paul Cuffee, who became a wealthy ship-owner in the US city of Boston, once put it succinctly when he said that pan-Africanism "fired the imagination of American freed slaves to return to the homeland and build a great nation".

Cuffee put one of his vessels at the service of those freed slaves who sailed back to Africa and settled in Sierra Leone. Later, the destination of a second group was Liberia. A number of ex-slave groups came from England, Nova Scotia and the West Indies to join comrades in Sierra Leone. In the 1920s, the Back to Africa Movement was again revived by Marcus Aurelius Garvey. He represented the most militant expression of the African nationalism in diaspora. Through his Back to Africa Movement, he not only made the blacks in the Western hemisphere conscious of their African origin but created for the first time a feeling of international solidarity among Africans and people of African descent. Garvey founded organizations to preach and spread his gospel of black Zionism. These were the Universal Negro Movement Associations and African Communities Imperial League. His chief slogan was "Africa for the Africans at home and abroad". His reason for deciding to build a mighty black nation came as a response to the black dilemma:

> Where is the black man's government? Where is his king and kingdom? Where is his president, his country and ambassador, his army, his navy, his men of big affairs?

On 1 August 1920, Garvey convened his first parliament which was attended by representatives "from far and wide". This date was deliberately chosen, because it was on 1 August 1834 that Queen Victoria had set free the slaves of the British empire. Garvey therefore selected this date to call together the descendants of those freed slaves "to proclaim the new struggle against the white man's oppression in Africa". He reflected on the feelings of his audience by the following exhortation:

> Wake up, Ethiopia, wake up Africa;
> Let's work towards the one, glorious, and a free, redeemed and mighty nation.
> Let Africa be a bright star among the constellation of nations.

It was Marcus Garvey who founded the Universal Africa Legion with the motto "One People! One aim! One destiny!" He was also responsible for other movements such as the Universal Black Cross Nurse, the Universal African Motto Corps and the Black Eagle Flying Corps. He established his own Africa Orthodox Church led by a black patriarch. He adopted the image of the "Black Christ". To publicize his ideas, he founded a publication by the name of *Negro World*. Some of his popular slogans were "Africa for Africans", "Renaissance of the Black Race" and "Ethiopia Awake!" Garvey's movement was hated by colonial powers, and the *Negro World* was banned in all colonial territories. Although the movement never achieved its aims and objectives, it had a transformative effect on African nationalism.

The second phase of the growth of the international black movement was dominated by W.E.B. Dubois, a distinguished scholar who was opposed to Garvey's strategies and therefore launched the idea of pan-Africanism as a rival political ideology to Garvey's black Zionism. The former was essentially anti-imperialist and non-racial but, as Dubois himself advocated, it was also for "complete government of Africans in Africa organized on the basis of socialism and cooperative economy, which would have no room for millionaires, black or white". His elements defining pan-Africanism were national self-determination, individual liberty and democratic socialism. The ultimate goal of pan-Africanism was the dream of founding a single, united state of Africa, but this aim was faced with obstacles of localized nationalism. In its more limited regional achievement, however, pan-Africanism has already led to the formation of one loose political union and several promising economic organizations spanning the continent. More important has been its contribution to the decolonization process in Africa. In the thought of Dubois, the idea of pan-Africanism as an intellectual enterprise was to achieve the cooperation among all groups of African descent in order to bring about "the industrial and spiritual emancipation of the Negro people".

It is interesting to note that various forms of African nationalism seem not to have been in harmony with a continental African agenda. Thus, at the level of a particular language group or greater tribe like the Yoruba in Nigeria, Kikuyu in Kenya or Xosa in South Africa, ethnic nationalism was predominant. In the political realm of the nation-state, the pulse of national identity was to be felt in the colours of the flag, the national anthem and particular symbols of national pride. Then regional identities such as East African Cooperation or Southern Africa Development Cooperation with particular histories and shared heritage came into play, and only beyond that there may be found a concept of unity of the continent.

At the third annual conference of the American Society of African Culture held in 1960 at the University of Pennsylvania, several speakers expressed conflicting opinions. Raymond Logan, a black American historian, saw pan-Africanism in terms of self-government by African countries south of Sahara, thus disagreeing with the Nigerian journalist and politician Chief Anthony Enahoro, who insisted that it included the economic, social and cultural development of the continent, the avoidance of conflict among African states, the promotion of African unity and influence in world affairs. According to Nnadi Azikiwe, first president of Nigeria, pan-Africanism connoted a situation which finds the whole continent of Africa free from the shackles of foreign domination with its leaders free to plan for the orderly progress and welfare of their people. The movement of pan-Africanism was another element in the struggle for political independence. Its African proponents also included Kwame Nkrumah, the first president of Ghana, black Africa's first country to gain independence in 1957. It was Nkrumah who, at a time when Christianity was misused to promote Western imperialism, referred to Jesus' words and coined the political slogan: "Seek ye first the political kingdom." For him, that was a key part of his passionate appeal for unity. The establishment of a united African "political kingdom" would, therefore, be the answer to future problems. Nkrumah was a dreamer; he had a vision. His cry for political unity in Africa could be heard wherever he spoke to his colleagues. They saw in him the protagonist of African nationalism. He foresaw that

> if we [Africans] do not unite, we will fight one another while the imperialists and neo-colonialists watch behind the scenes and secretly pull the strings with which we will cut each other's throats.

Kwame Nkrumah, *Africa Must Unite*, p.17

Nkrumah's vision stemmed from his personal experience. He had seen how the United Africa Company robbed his country of all resources and how the people in the Gold Coast (modern-day Ghana) were left to starve during the economic crisis.

The independence struggle

The desire to attain political unity and economic independence led to the formation of the United Nations Economic Commission for Africa (ECA) in Addis Ababa in 1958 and later to the formation of the Organization for African Unity (OAU) in 1963. In the following year, the African Development Bank (ADB) was established in Abidjan, Ivory Coast.

However, these organizations were not really animated by the spirit of pan-Africanism. During the silver jubilee of the OAU in 1988, there was nothing to celebrate, only misery to harvest. The OAU has been known to be a "toothless bulldog" engaged in the rhetoric of "unity in progress" without the instruments to effect any responses to the conflicts that are rampant in Africa. The OAU has been perceived to be an exclusive club for African heads of state and government who engage in cheap politics and make many empty promises. But one of the main reasons for its establishment was to create a forum through which a consensus on matters regarding unity among African states could be reached – something like a secular ecumenical council. Of course, this unity could not be achieved without the active involvement in the fight for freedom by all African states.

On 15 August 1994, African heads of state met in Arusha, Tanzania, to conclude the activities of the OAU freedom committee following Nelson Mandela's presidential victory in South Africa. With the end of formal apartheid, Africa has attained political freedom and thereby achieved the objective of the freedom committee.

During this meeting, Sir Ketumile Masire, the president of Botswana, stated, in reference to the speech given by Kenya's president Daniel arap Moi, that post-colonial Africa had been destroyed by the terrible failure of its leaders. Africa had to free itself from this self-destructive kind of leadership which had led to the abuse of human rights and democratic principles. President Masire charged that after the dissolution of the freedom committee of the OAU, Africa needed national leadership that could react to the needs of its people and also be dissolved by democratic means. He reiterated that a responsible opposition and press as well as the whole electorate were integral parts of the process of democratic leadership. President Masire repeated that African leaders had become money-hungry, intolerant and selfish. Most of the leaders were ready to do anything just to attain their egoistic goals. These leaders would drive their own people to ethnic animosity in order to stay in power. He emphasized that this was, however, political shortsightedness of the worst form because once ethnic violence had been stirred it could not easily be reversed. He stressed that the OAU should strengthen its mechanisms for preventing, processing and solving conflicts as well as establish an OAU peace commission with a permanent financial foundation just like the dissolved freedom committee.

The president of Botswana simply told his colleagues that black Africa had now entered a different phase in its fight for freedom. The fight must now be directed towards internal structures of oppression. The idea of freedom from colonialism was not – to describe it by a picture – to have a fox at loose in a chicken-run. No, the fox must be tamed. Pan-Africanism failed to achieve this taming. With the end of the OAU mandate to establish sovereign states, a new era of "second liberation" had dawned in Africa.

Even Kwame Nkrumah, a man with a great dream, became a victim of his own thirst for power. In order to keep his dream alive, Nkrumah had many people who criticized his policies put behind bars. He compounded his guilt through his style of governance, and the enemies he had created later betrayed him. He was overthrown in 1966 and later died in exile. Ali Mazrui, in *The African Condition*, maintains the view that many prominent African liberators, including Nkrumah, had a vision but not the necessary experience to lead a new country, because they inherited all sorts of problems that were further aggravated externally. In fact, most colonial powers still wielded a lot of influence at the time African countries became independent. This was mainly through the control of the economic and financial systems, but Nkrumah believed that independence involved sovereign states free both from economic dependency or political entanglements. He saw continental unity as a solution to Africans' weak position in the world system. Nkrumah felt the need to go beyond political or economic freedom, to achieve an independence from the ethical and aesthetic standards of the West, to affirm age-old indigenous traditions, customs and values in a modern world. It was a natural impulse, a desire to be rid of alien colonial ways in education, language, art and philosophy. It involved a desire to introduce an authentic African idiom into the mainstream of contemporary world civilization. Nkrumah concluded, "A union of African states will raise the dignity of Africa and strengthen its impact on world affairs. It will make possible the full expression of the African personality."

Socialism and autonomy

Like Nkrumah, Mwalimu Julius Nyerere held a view of independence that was forward-looking, and many of his ideas were deeply rooted in a form of socialism. He turned to the African past for justification of the democratic egalitarian socialist society he envisioned for the Tanzanian people. Nyerere abhorred the individualistic, self-seeking acquisitive and hedonistic character of capitalism, and like Léopold Sédar Senghor, the first president of Senegal, he rejected the bureaucratic socialism of Eastern Europe for he could not accept the communist doctrine of class conflict in Africa. Nyerere therefore turned to communal socialism as an expression of pan-Africanism based on community solidarity as a way of life in which wealth was produced and shared by all.

Nyerere's personal view of a modern Africa emerged as a juxtaposition of the old and the new. He was committed to promoting an African socialism based on an ethic by which each individual places social welfare ahead of personal profit. Accordingly, Africans were seen to have no more need for being "converted" to socialism than we have of being "taught" democracy. Both are rooted in the past and present experience of life in the traditional society. Nyerere realized that his people came to recognize that the same socialist attitude of mind which in the tribal days gave to every individual the security that comes from belonging to a widely extended family must today be preserved within the still wider society of the nations. It was thought by some to be "trouble-making" for Julius Nyerere, years before national flags were hoisted over new sovereign states, to look ahead and recommend steps in preparation for an East African federation of Uganda, Kenya, Tanganyika. And it was thought to be "idealistic chatter" for nationalist movements in 1958 to launch a regional organization, the Pan-African Freedom Movement of East and Central Africa, aiming first at independence and then at federation.

After Julius Nyerere had led his country to independence in 1961, he developed a unique form of African socialism using the concept of *ujamaa*. In 1967, Tanzania declared itself a socialist country after passing the Arusha Declaration. With the slogan "socialism and autonomy", an explicit commitment to socialism was endorsed. The concept of "autonomy" was construed as the freedom to carry out development projects without depending on assistance from the government or from outside. The concept of "socialism" was interpreted differently. State control over decision-makers in the economy was rated positively. Immediately after the declaration, all banks and insurance firms as well as nearly all sisal plantations, cereal mills and the Tanzanian assets of seven multinational companies were nationalized de facto.

But the concept of "socialism" also implied that there should no longer be certain other phenomena like exploitation, corruption and the establishment of a class society. The party decreed that its leaders (senior government officials, managers of state corporations and party functionaries) were no longer allowed to have more than one source of income, lease out property or sit on administrative boards of private companies. The political leaders, including the president, lowered their salaries and the ministers could no longer use their official vehicles for private business. Nyerere emphasized the moral aspects of his theory and, in *Freedom and Socialism*, stressed that "socialism was a mode of living and a socialist society could not be created out of nothing. It could only be created by those who believe in socialist ideas and translate the principles of socialism into action."

Nyerere did not see development simply as the acquisition of national wealth or the creation of a new infrastructure. He repeatedly emphasized that for a nation that had been enslaved, oppressed, exploited and humiliated through colonialism or capitalism, "development" meant nothing other than "liberation". Everything which accords the people greater control over their own affairs is a step towards better development, even if this is not automatically accompanied by better health or more bread. He pleaded passionately for an independent African model of democracy and socialism, arguing that in settling for its own type of democracy Tanzania rejected the Western model. It was Nyerere's firm conviction that *ujamaa* was best suited to guard the sovereignty of the people while guaranteeing an effective and strong government at the same time, which was vital at the stage of Tanzania's development in the mid-1960s. For him, it was also a question of maintaining dignity in that Africans must refuse to be dictated to, either by the West or the Eastern bloc, when it comes to the issues of governance. The Tanzanian approach represents an important process towards self-confidence which is critical to any genuine emancipation of a people emerging from a protracted state of colonialism.

Tanzania is now one of the most stable countries in Africa, both politically and otherwise. Besides the national pride promoted by a common linguistic culture – Swahili is spoken almost everywhere and the level of illiteracy is very low – the political awareness of the people is highly developed. Salim Ahmed Salim, a former deputy prime minister of Tanzania and former general secretary of the Organization of African Unity, is convinced that Tanzania represents a success story of struggle against the negative historical influence of colonialism and its modern version, neo-colonialism. It is also a successful example of a genuine attempt to find lasting solutions to the African crisis. In the face of globalization and the formation of trade and political blocs in the European Union, the Americas and Asia, it is envisaged that the newly formed African Union will push for favourable trade relations with the rest of the world. The AU will initiate rapid responses to future conflicts, negotiate better terms of trade and develop a common position for African countries in world affairs.

The African Union, which was inaugurated in Durban, South Africa, on 9 July 2002, faces many challenges. Perhaps the most daunting one is how to maintain unity in a heavily balkanized continent. The AU will have to reimagine the place and meaning of territorial boundaries which hitherto have constituted the greatest hindrance to the movement of people, goods and ideas between and across the countries of Africa. The logic, motivation and purpose of the existing boundaries are antithetical to everything the AU stands for.

The colonial legacy

Around 1880, at a time when there was nationalistic euphoria in Europe, Belgium, France, England, Germany, Portugal and Spain began to wrangle bitterly for the partition of the "African cake". The French and the British obtained parts of Congo, Central Africa and the West African coast. The French left to the Belgians the regions to the left of Congo, while they took the regions to the right of the river. The Germans, who until then had not acquired any territories, joined hands with the French in order to prevent the British from "ruling the whole world". Great Britain united with Portugal to prevent Germany and France from "destroying world peace". Portugal grabbed Angola and Mozambique, while the British took the region around the Great River Limpopo (modern-day Zimbabwe, South Africa and Botswana). The bitter rivalries between the European states led to the Berlin conference (1884-85) at which the Europeans agreed on the partitioning of the African continent among themselves. That is how the continent became a source of raw materials for European industrialization. With the partitioning of Africa into territories ruled and controlled by the colonial powers, a process of plundering of human and natural resources began – from whose effects Africa still suffers.

According to the Ghanaian historian Adu Boahen, the European states colonized Africa mainly to establish new markets for their finished products, to find a steady source of raw materials, to invest their surplus capital and to maintain prestige and power. The establishment of an infrastructure for the transportation of goods, an administrative system – and even an education system – were all meant to serve the economic gains of the colonial regime. In this way, nations were formed which, owing to their links with Europe, could hardly survive upon gaining independence.

The poverty and disorientation in most African countries have their roots in the disorganization of this earlier period, when Africa was the playground of the European powers. At the end of the second world war, most Africans did not want to fight for the freedom of the "whites" any longer, only to be deprived of their own. They had not fought to save the world from Hitler and then continue to be victims of British, French, Belgian and Portuguese oppression. It is this particular consciousness brought about by the war in Europe that led to the birth of the independence movement in Africa.

In a speech read during the British peace congress in October 1949, Nnadi Azikiwe (the first president of Nigeria) pointed out that the British, who claimed to have fought in the world war with the sole aim of rescuing Europe from tyranny and dictatorship, had subjected the Nigerian people to the same tyranny. Patrice Lumumba, who led Congo, the modern-day Democratic Republic of Congo, to independence, publicly rebuked the Belgians and criticized the exploitation of the Congolese people. In Senegal, women led by Ramatoulaye and Penda defied the French absolute authority and marched to Dakar, the modern-day Senegalese capital, in order to support their husbands who were on strike. In East Africa there was a fierce military uprising against the British – the Mau-Mau movement.

The independence movement in Africa mainly demanded the restoration of human rights and freedom. These included land ownership, the right to education, the freedom of movement and human dignity. All the pioneers of African nationalism expressed the wish for self-rule. Jomo Kenyatta, who later became the first president of Kenya, had often expressed in public meetings the desire for African unity. It became very clear from the Mau-Mau revolts that the independence movement accompanied its words with actions. One of the Mau-Mau fighters once said, "I vow to sacrifice my life in the fight for independence of the nation and expect no pay – apart from our freedom." During one of the election campaigns of the Kenya African National Union (KANU) led by Kenyatta, a flag was raised as a symbol of African rule. The red colour at the centre, symbolizing human blood, was surrounded by black and green. Kenyatta is said to have told his followers that "the tree of freedom can grow only if blood, and not water, is poured onto it". The fertile land, symbolized by the green colour on the flag, could only be acquired through the blood of Africans (red and black).

Kenyatta demanded freedom of speech, freedom of movement and freedom of the press for the Africans. He made it clear to his people that apart from the freedom of religion, all the other forms of freedom were not given to them. Many Africans were prosecuted for trespassing onto the white man's land or into an area of the city that was out of bounds for them. For the Mau-Mau, there was no greater sacrifice than giving one's life for the nation and watering the tree of freedom with one's blood. This spirit of personal commitment to the fight for self-determination also marked the road to freedom in South Africa. In his famous defence speech during the Rivonia trial which began in October 1963, Nelson Mandela said:

> During my youth in the Transkei, I would listen to the stories of our tribal elders whenever they narrated stories of the old times. I was particularly impressed by the reports about the battles our forefathers fought to defend their home. I hoped then that life would give me the opportunity to serve my people and person-

ally make a modest contribution to the fight for freedom. Those were the motives behind what I did and for which I now stand accused before this court...

But most of all, we want equal political rights because without them there will be no change from our disadvantaged position. I know that this sounds revolutionary in the ears of the whites in this country because the majority of the voters will be Africans. That is why the white man fears democracy... I have dedicated my life to the struggle of the African people. I have fought against white domination and against black domination. I have cherished the ideal of a democratic and free society in which all people live together in peace and with equal opportunities. I will live for this ideal and hope to attain it. If need be, it is an ideal for which I am prepared to die.

> A detailed analysis of the trial and the famous speech
> by Mandela can be found in
> *Nelson Mandela*, by Meredith Martin, pp.248-80

African humanity

At the same time that movements for political independence were being born, there emerged an intense desire for cultural emancipation, African self-determination and political and economic unity of the African people. The movement for cultural emancipation was mainly expressed in the works of African poets and philosophers such as Aimé Césaire, Frantz Fanon and Léopold Sédar Senghor. The concept of "negritude" – a return to the cultural traditions of the black people as well as the demand for the abolition of colonialism – was coined by Aimé Césaire in the early 1930s. Negritude was the emphasizing of the uniqueness and strengths of African humanity as opposed to Western individualism.

Léopold Sédar Senghor, the poet and philosopher who later became the first president of Senegal in 1960, acclaimed negritude as the humanism of the 20th century. He stressed that negritude was neither racism nor self-negation, rather it was an establishment by itself and a self-confirmation of African identity. Joseph Nyasani, a professor of philosophy at the university of Nairobi, once said that this mixed culture has turned the African elite into "non-critical zombies..., a fact that has led to a dilemma as far as their dignity, their social visions and development strategies are concerned". By copying Western life-styles and values, they distanced themselves from a critical participation in the development processes in their own rural communities. Having been influenced by colonial systems of education, the African elite could not really understand how cultural estrangement and its contradictions hampered development efforts and social advancement. The destruction of traditional ways of thinking and the lack of a critical reflection of what it means to be an African has produced half-baked professionals who want to use Western analytical methods in describing and prescribing solutions to the problems of the continent.

Nevertheless the idea of "tribe", a concept that has endeared itself to Western scholars and journalists for a century, is primarily a means to reduce for readers the complexity of the indigenous non-Western societies of Africa, Asia, South America, North America and the Pacific. It is no accident that the contemporary uses of the term tribe were developed during the 19th-century rise of evolutionary and racist theories to designate alien non-white peoples as inferior or less civilized and as having not yet evolved from a simpler, primal state. The uses and definitions of "tribe" in the sociological and anthropological literature are varied and conflicting; some authors mean common language, others common culture, some ancestral lineages, and others common government or rulers. More disturbing were the political use of the term by the Rhodesian and South African apartheid governments to legitimize opposition movements and by journalists as a code of disorganized, primitive and less civilized peoples. This has been seen in previous descriptions of the Zimbabwean Patriotic Front liberation movements ZAPU and ZANU as "tribally based" movements – in academic journals, the network evening news, the *New York Times* and even the *Smithsonian Magazine*. Accordingly, ZANU represents the Shona tribe and ZAPU the Ndebele tribe. In fact, a majority of the ZAPU cadres are not Ndebele-speaking soldiers but speak Shona and Sotho dialects. Indeed, the ZAPU leader Joshua Nkomo was not Ndebele but Karanga in rural origin. ZANU, on the other hand, has a majority of Zezuru, Ndau, Manica, Karanga and other Shona-family dialects, none of whom share common chiefs or rulers. ZANU has also Ndebele-speakers and other members from non-Shona dialects.

In fact, the turmoil in Zimbabwe has been primarily between different political parties with differing histories, leaderships, styles, goals and memberships – differences which should be well-known to members of political parties and religious organizations in Western nations. These different party organizations help to "create" these ethnic, not tribal, identities in the same way that the ward organizations and politicians of 19th- and 20th-century America fostered the Irish-American, Italian-American, Jewish-American and, later, black-American ethnic identities. In the same manner, being an ethnic Irish-American and the wearing of the green in New York became more important than being an Irishman in the old country before immigrating. Similarly in Africa, persons who never identified as Shona in the rural areas but as members of a particular village or lineage or family suddenly find Shona identities in the rough and tumble of urban politics. In New York, we term it ethnicity but in Africa it becomes tribalism.

Misperceiving and misnaming ethnicity in Africa, however, is not a small error. As the Confucian *Analects* of circa 500 BC note, "If names be not correct, language is not in accordance with the truth of things. If language is not in accordance with the truth of things, affairs cannot be carried on to success." Misnaming African ethnicity as tribalism has long bedevilled US foreign policy in Africa, leading to miscalculations and errors of judgment. According to David Wile, "When we respond to a political movement as only a tribal reality, we misjudge its strength, its potential organization, and the breadth of its appeal, as we clearly did in labelling as tribal groups the three political liberation movements of Angola."

Change and reality in politics

There has hardly been any African country in recent times, apart from Tanzania and Mali, which strives to develop a national philosophy in order to deal with the African legacy and its way of thinking and values. Kenya's former president, Daniel arap Moi, claims to have introduced a national philosophy generally known as "Nyayo" (the Swahili word for "footsteps") in order to promote "love, peace and unity" among the people of Kenya. However, this appears to be the kind of empty sloganeering meant to appeal to cultures of affection and a weak conscience. For it is under the emblem of political love that ethnic hatred, insecurity and political assassinations took place in Kenya. The uneasy peace was safeguarded by terrifying police brutality in a country in which "small tribes" are united against "big tribes". The language of political affection was used to win voters, the message of peace to attract foreign investors, and unity to serve the intention of clinging to power at all costs. The ideological vacuum in Africa can be traced to a style of leadership which not only serves foreign interests but also reflects ideological bankruptcy.

After a long struggle, the Moi government finally gave in and revoked clause two of the constitution, thereby opening the way for the registration of other political parties. However, a critical look at the change reveals that it was very superficial indeed. It is true that by removing the offending clause the constitutional arrangements adopted allowed for registration of more political parties. It is equally true, though, that by removing the clause there was no change in the social conditions. Similar political ideas were simply spread over several political parties of similar ideology and interests. The difference was in the rhetoric and polemics but not in the quality of the content. The same people who yesterday were in the ruling party KANU (Kenya African Union) became DP (Democratic Party), FORD (Forum for Restoration of Democracy), etc., overnight. In fact, if you dig deeper, you will unearth the truth: that about 99 percent of the leadership of the opposition political parties were life members of KANU. That means the motivation for changing from the ruling party to the opposition parties was not to fight for meaningful social change. Rather, it was to increase the chances of attaining positions.

A great deal of resources, energies and creative imagination were invested in fighting to win elections. The people were important only in so far as they could usher the politicians into parliament and other positions of importance. From the point of view of the politicians, the people had only one precious thing, the vote. In that respect, the quality of the relationships between the politician and the voter was the same with politicians both of the ruling party and the opposition. Sadly enough, this situation is a repeat of what happened at the time of independence a generation ago. In the mind of the political leaders, the change was not about political emancipation. Nor was it about transformation of socio-political relations. It was about taking over power. The ultimate goal of each political party was to capture the state house, the seat of power. The power relations between the politician and the people were to remain the same. The state apparatus, too, was to be kept intact. One has only to look critically at the election manifesto of the political parties, both the opposition and the ruling party.

Their essence is similar. To bring about meaningful democratic change in Africa, it will be critical to introduce a moral dimension, hitherto completely overlooked. The democracy we seek must be concerned not just with the electoral matters, but with the economic conditions of the majority of the people. It has to be a democracy that considers the unnecessary suffering of the people as being morally wrong and therefore unacceptable. The lack of creativity among African leaders has led to a situation where decisions on matters affecting the public are left to politicians who assume absolute authority. This is the context of today's dilemma and dreams of pan-Africanism.

In concluding these reflections on the winding route of pan-Africanism, it seems appropriate to borrow the words of Marcus Garvey and his observation that it shall not be the politicians who will resolve this dilemma but the ordinary people of Africa:

> The time has come for the Negro to forget and cast behind him his hero worship and adoration of other races, and to start out immediately to create and emulate heroes of his own. We must canonize our own saints, create our own martyrs, and elevate to positions of fame and honour black men and women who have made their distinct contributions to our racial history. Sojourner Truth is worthy of the place of sainthood alongside Joan of Arc; Crispus Attucks and George William Gordon are entitled to the halo of martyrdom with no less glory than that of the martyrs of any other race. Toussaint L'Ouverture's brilliancy as a soldier and statesman outshone that of a Cromwell, Napoleon and Washington; hence, he is entitled to the highest place as a hero among men. Africa has produced countless numbers of men and women, in war and in peace, whose lustre and bravery outshine that of any other people. Then why not see good and perfection in ourselves?... We are entitled to our own opinions and not obligated to or bound by the opinions of others... The world today is indebted to us for the benefits of civilization. They stole our arts and sciences from Africa. Then why should we be ashamed of ourselves?

> "African Fundamentalism"

The relational dimensions must be on the agenda of the democracy we seek for Africa. For Africa, the community is a social tapestry of relationships which sustain the life of each and all the members of the community. The African traditional philosophy defines the being of the individual as meaningful only in relation to the others. Outside of such interwoven relations, the individual person, however materially rich, is actually a nobody. "To be" is to be in good relationships with others in the community. Such understanding of the quality of being ought to be built into the vision of democracy for Africa. Where such a situation prevails, the commodification of the vote, now rampant in the current democratic systems, will be totally alien.

The church in Africa has a major social responsibility in the democratization process in Africa. The church should seek to promote democracy as a vision whose basic elements are freedom, equality, justice and fullness of life. It is in this respect that the church will contribute to the articulation of the second prong of the vision of pan-Africanism: the spiritual and economic emancipation of the African people.

4. Migration of the European Nation-State in Africa

> The emphasis on differentiation meant the forging of specifically "native" institutions through which to rule subjects. But the institutions so defined and enforced were not racial as much as ethnic, not "native" as much as "tribal". Racial duality was thereby anchored in a politically enforced ethnic dualism.
>
> Mahmood Mamdani, *Citizen and Subject*, p.7

In this chapter, we shall explore the various dimensions of the crisis of the European nation-state model in Africa as an act of indignity and how a free Europe became the beacon of oppression on the continent. Subsequent to the partition and scramble for Africa, the next stage in the formation of nascent nation-states was characterized by brief periods of turbulence and struggles for self-determination. Essentially, Africa remained part of Europe in the use of language, public delivery systems, structures of governance and pedagogy. The general analysis of the trends on the continent seems to point towards pessimism and despondency, especially when Western forms of liberal democracy, perceived as the universal model of governance, were regarded as the acme of modernity. Hence, the African experience and appropriation of the European mode of governance during and after colonial domination is a critical question indeed.

This overview will help us engage in an exercise of discernment and understanding why the spirit of pessimism endures even in the context of the promises of the emerging *global order* (expressed in italics because the notion of globalization itself is contaminated with ideological contradictions which undermine modernization; e.g., intolerance to diversity, bureaucratization and consolidation of power in the name of democracy). This sense of pessimism endures because of the void created by various invading ideologies on the continent of Africa. Despite impressions of a bleak future and an eroded past, Africa retains a rich reservoir of human authenticity. Paradoxically, this is deeply signified by conditions of estrangement and human suffering that have been largely ignored by history. And as the poet laments:

When all our hopes are sown on stony ground
And we have yielded up the thought of gain,
Long after our last songs have lost their sound
We may come back; we may come back again.

When thorns have choked the last green thing we loved
And have said all there is to say,
When love that moved us once leaves us unmoved
Then men and women like us may come to have a day.

For it will be with us as with the bee,
The meagre ant, the sea-gull and the loon
We may come back to triumph mournfully
An hour or two, but it will not be soon

Arna Botemps, "A Note of Humility"

We are witnessing a kind of political and economic dispensation that is linked to the Europeanization of Africa and the Africanization of European institutions in Africa. We are therefore confronted with the problems of authenticity and legitimacy. The former is indicative of the fact that the historical progression of the nation-state in the continent was not rooted; therefore, it does not reflect the soul of Africa. The issue of legitimacy has to do with the question of consent given that the people of Africa did not give and so do not participate fully in the state. An exercise in ethical discernment is therefore indispensable in confronting the dual dilemma of the so-called disfunctionality and disorderliness of the state in Africa.

There are other issues to be addressed, as outlined in the foregoing chapters: why the contemporary neo-liberal features of governance, namely multi-partyism, independent judicial system, free public press and popular legislative process, are contentious and occasionally have been a recipe for conflict instead of popular consent. The pitfalls and reversals of market-driven political reforms indicate the deepening of this dilemma. Yet this represents not so much the dilemma of conformity but the dilemma of authentic alternatives to neo-liberalism.

The nation-state in Africa

The road not taken (Basil Davidson's phraseology) and Mamdani's *Citizen and Subject* are the closest means to understanding the ideological content of this dilemma. Both demonstrate the features of the modern African nation-state remaining intricately linked to the "grand designs" of the colonial state. Davidson's thesis is that the predicament of Africa is "the curse of the nation-state".

Even so, in retrospect, it is bound to seem strange that the whole project of nation-statism, of promoting nationalism as a means of promoting nation-states, was so little inspected by the British authorities. The French, of course, could and did argue that they were not promoting nation-statism in "their Africa", but instead the elevation of their colonies to membership in *la plus Grande France;* the only nationalism promoted in those colonies would have to be French nationalism. But the British in authority ardently believed in the project of African nation-statism. "The objectives of our colonial policy have been summed up in a number of different formulae," affirmed Sir Hilton Poynton, a former administrative head of the British colonial office, speaking in 1978 after a long and successful career, "but the shortest and simplest is 'nation-building'." And by this, Sir Hilton clearly meant the "building" of separate nation-states as the successors and inheritors of colonial states.

The nation-state in its current form and substance, especially in Africa, must be subject to an ethical critique. How does the nation-state respond or correspond to the question of human dignity? What are the ethical criteria for its existence? Is the nation-state absolutely the necessary institution that alone guarantees organizing for sustenance of life on planet earth? It is within the context of the African experience that we seek to comprehend the meaning of the nation-state and why it should exist at all. We then have to examine its features and genealogy before we can begin to imagine alternatives. Furthermore, as has been noted, not all the Africans tried to found states.

Other crucial questions that arise have to do with possible ethical foundations upon which a renewed form of the nation-state may be derived. We need to examine carefully the ideological basis of the nation-state in Africa and how bureaucratization of power through feudalism found its way into and was mingled with the parallel modernization in Africa. Other forms of bureaucracies and systems of managing public resources were not alien to Africa. For example, the Pharaonic state was bureaucratic, not feudal. Its great title-holders were officials, not hereditary territorial magnates who had been incorporated within a larger unity. The largest triumph of the Pharaohs was fiscal. By using to the full the arts of the scribe, the surveyor and the tax collector, they channelled the surplus production of the flood plain into one set of coffers. Some individuals and some religious corporations were exempt from tax; but only royal officials collected the revenue and mobilized labour for civil and military purposes.

The architects of modern colonial rule intended to design a system in which the colonial state itself entrenched its hegemonic project within the historical context of its subjects, utilizing authoritarian structures and introducing new modes of tyranny that classified communities and peoples into subordinate identities.

The bifurcated state, as well described by Mahmood Mamdani, projected a dual identity; i.e., rural Africa was under the pretext of self-rule of an appointed local chief while the urban area was managed under the command of white officials. In the case of the latter, direct rule was exercised through "modern rule of law" to inculcate the European values of "civility" and "modernity" – which constituted what is referred to as centralized despotism. With regard to the former, indirect rule was applied through customary law with ethnically defined native authorities; this constituted decentralized despotism. This bifurcation of the state is what led to the clashing identities of village elite in the city and their rural counterparts who were subjects. Thus, the progressive migration of the European state led to market-based identities in relationships between the settler communities and the natives, so that even when the peasants incorporated into the state as subjects ethnically, once they crossed the social boundaries from rural areas to the urban environment, they were racially excluded from becoming citizens in the city.

Neither institutional segregation nor apartheid was a South African invention. If anything, both idealized a form of rule that the British colonial office dubbed "indirect rule" and the French *association*. Three decades before Jan Smuts, Lord Lugard had pioneered indirect rule in Uganda and Nigeria. And three decades after Smuts, Lord Hailey would sum up the contrast between forms of colonial rule as turning on a distinction between "identity" and "differentiation" in organizing the relationship between Europeans and Africans:

> The doctrine of identity conceives the future social and political institution of Africans as destined to be basically similar to those of Europeans; the doctrine of differentiation aims at the evolution of separate institutions appropriate to African conditions and differing both in spirit and in form from those of Europeans.

> Lord Hailey, *An African Survey*, p.150

The role of the European nation-state in creating new political and economic arrangements for the exploitation of both human and natural resources in Africa must always be highlighted if we are to have a clear portrait of Africa as it is today. The colonial regime primarily designed the state as an instrument of manipulation and control of the movement of people and goods to create and secure wealth. Thus, the process of statecraft was essentially a process of corruption not only of indigenous institutions but also of the general polity. At the heart of it all, Africa has remained captive not only to the hobbled nature of her legal independence which survived the struggle for autonomy but also, and more critically, to the transfer or migration of the concept and practices of the European nation-state into Africa.

Governance and conflict

The nature and origin of conflicts in the recent history of the continent of Africa can be summarized as the outcome of a frustrated and fragmented transition to the so-called modern nation-state amid the vestiges of imperialism and colonial rule. The issue of political and economic woes in contemporary Africa could never be treated in isolation from conditions that are deeply rooted in a history full of paradox and the impact of a sustained global invasion of the continent that will linger on for many years to come. The purpose of this chapter is to transcend particular episodes and begin to explore further the features of the African nation-state and its European origin as a process of historical and cultural migration. In later chapters, we shall explore the global context in which the African nation-state struggles for identity and the subtle responses to the issues posed by the problems of post-modernism as they relate to Africa.

Much of the politics taking place in Africa today is found outside formal structures of state institutions. The corporate imaging of the state does not necessarily reflect the inner logic and life of the state as a public institution, and that is why classical analytical instruments premised upon certain institutional paradigms tend to be defective. There are "hidden" forms of the identity of the state in Africa that are difficult to discern, not because they are informal in nature but because they are subtle manifestations of the amorphous and transitional moment in which the state functions amid the fluidity of power.

The post-colonial, patrimonial systems of governance in Africa are a cultural enhancement of a defective translation (or should we say transplantation) of a crisis-ridden, European nation-state model into Africa. Contemporary absence of structural differentiation between state-related institutions, civil society and the general polity may be traced back to the origin and nature of migration of intermediary forms of the European nation-state and feudal structures of governance into Africa. The problem of private European boundaries which redefined, as part of a new polity, various ethnic nationalities that had existed in their own right posed a dilemma for Africa. The problem of this distinction is further complicated by the appropriation and misappropriation (at the same time) of the indigenous governance infrastructures into European modes of exploitation on the continent. These of course are signified by the classic models of the British and French policies in Africa; i.e. indirect rule and assimilation (which will be examined in greater detail in the following chapters).

Furthermore, the political mapping of the continent by European powers at the Berlin conference is what essentially initiated the invention of the contemporary nation-state in Africa. The feudal space in Europe then became public space in Africa, and so the boundaries remained contaminated with vested interests and expansionist policies that had nothing to do with the basic considerations of values and ethical systems in African communities. The claim of innocence on the part of Africa applies to ordinary people who have endured under the burden of a model of the state that was imposed upon them by foreigners. The ethical dimensions of indigenous systems and structures of governance are in captivity to a failure of historical memory because the contemporary institutions ignore their existence and function.

The state itself has remained a device of control and manipulation by those in power. The clients of the state are not the ordinary citizens but middle persons who deliver promises of loyalty from the polity to the head of state. This involves complex relations based on patriarchal systems and structures of authority that connect the clients of the state to patrons both at the local and national levels. But these structures are no longer hinged on the value systems upon which they were originally anchored – the communitarian ethic of equanimity and the preservation of the kindred spirit to ensure the growth and well-being of all members within the community.

Under the current geopolitical arrangements in Africa, the question of ascertaining legitimacy therefore becomes difficult if not impossible, especially with regard to the way and manner in which the nation-state is constructed. The participation of the people in the formation of the state and management of public resources remains problematic due both to the personalized and informal nature of nation-state clientelism and to the colonial origin of its historical development. As I will endeavour to demonstrate, the coming of the nation-state was not only a false start in Africa but also a crime against Africa.

The causal significance of the formation of the modern European nation-state was not congenial to values and norms of the African communal states. The European mentality which is the product of the struggles and eventual maturation of a system of capital accumulation could not be successfully assimilated into the ethical domain of the pre-colonial African communal systems of governance. The positive growth and development of the modern European nation-state required the emancipation of the public sphere from the control and monopoly of the internal feudal and imperial regimes.

While it is equally true that the emergence and development of the African nation-state also requires her emancipation from internal patrimonial systems and structures that undermine democracy, the truth is that the continent has yet to be emancipated from the tyranny of the modern nation-state. There is a confluence of both local and global forms of tyranny that are linked historically from the post-colonial to the global project of the 1980s.

So the state in Africa is under siege because of its own history and the global condition, such that public displays of the strength of the state in Africa are symbolic of the modes of tyranny that it has successfully borrowed from the European imposed nation-state. The open displays of military might to the public during state functions and the pervasive culture of secrecy function as reminders of the nation-state as a private institution that is massively equipped to exercise power and control over its people. The undemocratic institutions within the nation-state itself are safeguarded from public accountability by virtue of the compelling need for auton-

omy from the polity. This compelling need for autonomy is
what characterized the feudal and monarchical systems of
tyranny in the colonial world. Frantz Fanon described it can-
didly thus:

> The colonial world is a world cut in two. The dividing line, the
> frontiers, are shown by barracks and police stations. In the
> colonies it is the policeman and the soldier who are the official,
> instituted go-betweens, the spokesman of the settler and his rule
> of oppression.

The Wretched of the Earth, p.29

The use of force by the colonial settlers as a means to
reinforce their foreign reign upon peasants in Africa was not
any different from the exercise of power the landlords had
over their subjects in England. Africa needed alternative
internal structures to reclaim its own cultures, the values of
dignified participation of all African people in a movement
towards the creation of new instruments of governance.

The emancipation of the state

Nevertheless, the undemocratic institutions that in the
end still determine the security or insecurity of the European
nation-state model seem to be the anchor of survival of the
state in Africa. Military expenditure arising from the illusion
of external aggression and internal instability over-ride the
basic needs of starving populations on the continent and elsewhere. These can be explained not just through a formal
understanding of the functions of the nation-state but also
how state power is exerted and celebrated as an inhumanly
constructed institution. It is the sphere of influence of state
power over constitutional principle that determines yet is
also shaped by *realpolitik* having nothing to do with formal
political arrangements but rather with elements of power
grasped by patrons and their clients.

The "logic" of power is what now continues to inhibit and
impede the much-needed immediate emancipation of the state
from the private, informal, external and internal, "mysterious",
patrimonial structures that are alienating the cultures and val-

ues of African communities. The gradual linking of the private to the public in the development of the European model of the nation-state in Africa progressively led not only to an unclear distinction of roles and regulations within the state itself, but also to further differentiation of various centres of power as means of regulating the functions of the state. While institutional disfunctionality becomes the norm and disorder the mode of state operation and logistics, democracy is defined by electoral episodes and moments in which politicians languish in the misery of loss and the arrogance of triumph.

It must quickly be noted here that the process of de-linking the private from the public sphere in the development of the European nation-state itself was not consistent with the ethics of universal suffrage as we have been made to believe. In most cases it was the outcome of bloody revolutions, and in others a schematic project of the ruling class to avert possible attempts at revolution. Certainly in the former cases, such as the French revolution, there was a complete overhaul not only of the feudal structures but total replacement of the monarchy. In the latter, such as the case of Great Britain, there was a careful blending of imperial loyalty with the progressive forces of modernity.

Yet, while the gradual emancipation of the state from the private realm was taking place in Europe, there was in Africa a systematic unleashing of the same institutions of tyranny to which Europe had been captive. Although the partitioning of Africa took place at a time when the European nation-state was still at an early stage of development, the colonial project was executed at the climax of the modernization of the nation-state in Europe. The question is how a free Europe could enslave other nations with the very tools of oppression it had rejected. If the project of democratizing the state meant reclaiming the state from the private hands of monarchs and landlords, how is it that the same norms of civility that freed Europe did not feature in their relation to other nations? After all, is not the project of civilizing other nations meant to impart the values of civility which brought freedom and modernity to Europe?

In other words, the struggle for emancipation of the state was a struggle signified by class contradictions within the particular Euro-ethnic societies. It could not be replicated or transferred on a moral basis alone. For the revolutionary forces of change to be replicated, there had to be an organic relationship between the oppressed in Europe and the oppressed in Africa. But this dilemma cannot be explained in terms of class distinctions and lack of existential and geographical connectivity among the poor and the oppressed in Europe and Africa alone. Missing from that equation is the factor of race. Here the boundaries of Marxist analysis and the European project of racial construction are clearly drawn. Herein lies the most disturbing factor in the history of cultural genocide – the ideological construction of race. Racism was at the heart of the project of European conquest in Africa. It was both a metaphysical and political conviction. Racial prejudice against Africans was not subtle, as it is today: it was a deeply held, well-articulated and openly proclaimed European public policy in Africa:

> The blacks in Africa must be directed and moulded by Europeans but they are indispensable as assistants to the latter... The Africans by themselves did not account for a single useful invention nor any usable technical discovery, no conquest that counts in the evolution of humanity, nothing that can compare to the accomplishments in the areas of culture and technology by Europeans or even Asians.
>
> Marcello Caetano, *Os Nativos na Economia Africana*, p.16

It is interesting to note that studies on colonialism and its effect on Africa, even among scholars from the continent, tend to downplay the fact of racism and instead highlight the exploitative dimensions of economic projects which are often distinguished from the institutions of the slave trade and slavery that preceded them. Part of the dilemma of black presence in world history is that black people all over the world live with the disparities of a dual, conflicting consciousness in terms of colonialized and racialized categories of human identity. It is this dilemma which is partly responsible for problems of solidarity among African communities on the continent and those in the diaspora. Questions of the "nature" and "meaning" of black existence – as if we are particular, concrete manifestations in historical context of the "other" – are critical as part of the journey of the common self-understanding of African people all over the world. The dilemma of being trapped in the construct of a social reality to which African people cannot relate, unless they become unconscious of who they really are, is at the heart of the crisis of black humanity.

Blacks overcome their historical alienation through their own recognition of their history, in which case there are at least two histories, or they lay claim to the historical through recognizing themselves in a way that is consistent with the history that has already emerged. The former affirms blackness; the latter marks its elimination. Attempts to escape the trap of the process of historical unconsciousness have often led to projects of nostalgia, yet attempts to be affirmed within the same realm of "enlightened modernity" are often disguised means of sanctioning the underlying evil of racism.

Modernity and race

The writing of this book may be out of practical necessity as an endeavour to engage in a recovery programme which does not situate black experience outside "modernity" but actually claims modernity as a product of African existence; at the same time, it is a critical venture which defies the ideological undergirdings of white supremacy in the construction of pre-modern and modern conceptualizations of Africa and the black world. Incidentally, in the USA the black presence still survives and thrives not by exclusion but inclusion in the very core and fabric of a matured, radicalized environment. As in post-colonial Africa, the subtleties of *race matters* are not just experienced in America but their structural and hidden forms exist everywhere in the traces of institutions left behind by a history of anti-black discrimination.

It seems that one must first address the notion of modernity itself (this is a subject that I wish to return to in chapter 6) in order to reveal the underlying lies of historians, yet not as if modernity were itself something alien to or outside of black experience. It is the embodiment of the contradictions of black presence as defined by European experience that raises the fundamental problems – as if to suggest that black existence came into being only when white Europeans appeared on the continent of Africa! It is a naïve and fallacious position to think that the history of the black race began only with European conquests. Yet this fallacy permeates the modern consciousness of most Europeans and Africans alike.

The everyday dimension of racism in society breeds a comfortable historiography of bad faith. Racist institutions are designed so as to facilitate racism as gracefully as walking through air on a calm summer's day. Reality is radicalized and rationalized with racist categories so as to permeate to the core of explanation.

It is, however, beyond the scope of our present discourse to engage the philosophical premises of black inclusion in "white modernity", but we shall deal with the terrible reign of tyranny and violence in the way the so-called "contractions of modernity" (ironically Western "civility" and values and their modern institutional embodiment) are being and have been "transferred" to non-Western African cultures under the aegis of the nation-state.

We cannot escape the ambivalence embodied in the contradictions this discourse represents; for example, African presence in history (both on the continent of Africa and in the diaspora) as a dilemma of being there and not being there at the same time. It is no longer a tragedy of complete absence, but of presence and absence together.

The establishment of colonialism was an act of cultural and political violence. Racial distinctions and ideological constructions are the corruption of God's creation. But for it to work, racism required local partners in Africa who were willing to collaborate. The intervening imperial powers had to corrupt some members and leaders in local communities in order to infiltrate the African hinterland and establish the infrastructure for "divide and rule".

It is interesting to note that contemporary theories of political development in Africa continue to focus on major impediments to modernization of the nation-state as if there were no historical basis for its disfunctionality on the continent. As a matter of fact, the historical basis for the development and growth of the European nation-state model is exploitation and oppression of other cultures and societies.

Cornel West best captures and articulates the process of cultural oppression:

> Needless to say, this fragile experiment began by taking for granted the ugly conquest of Amerindians and Mexicans, the exclusion of women, the subordination of European working-class men and the closeting of homosexuals. These realities made many of the words of the revolutionary Declaration of Independence ring a bit hollow. Yet the enslavement of Africans – over 20 percent of the population – served as the linchpin of American democracy; that is, the much-heralded stability and continuity of American democracy was predicated upon black oppression and degradation. Without the presence of black people in America, European-Americans would not be "white" – they would be only Irish, Italians, Poles, Welsh and others engaged in class, ethnic and gender struggles over resources and identity. The scenario is classically Hobbesian ("the sovereign can reign so long as it is able to protect those who live within its will"), a notion that enables sovereignty to extend way beyond its borders. By the time we arrive at Antonio Gramsci... – from 1776 to 1964, 188 years of our 218-year history – this racial divide would serve as a basic presupposition for the expansive functioning of American democracy, even as the concentration of wealth and power remained in the hands of a few well-to-do white men.

Cornel West, *Race Matters*, p.156

The ethical basis for the existence of the state as a public institution in its current form (privatization or racial individualization of the state) must now be questioned seriously even when an alternative language, relevant to the future of Africa, must be sought. Here, I wish to re-emphasize that during the cold war the state in Africa, under the siege of bipolar power contests, became increasingly a private institution. The revolutionary forces that were released in the protracted struggles against colonial rule were soon dissipated by sponsored political assassinations and installation of military and/or civilian dictatorial regimes. Elsewhere, moderate leadership that sought to rescue the continent through the non-aligned movement either became compromised or frustrated. When the state becomes a private corporate enterprise, then surely it is paving the way to another project of colonial proportions, this time under the guise of globalization. Racism, therefore, is to be found in mutual reinforcement of local tyranny and structures of the state in Africa.

Transplanting the nation-state

The school of thought that best articulates the predicament and struggle of racial estrangement in African politics is expressed in the works of Frantz Fanon. It was the coming to terms with this political estrangement through the encounter between African students who went to Europe and the USA in the earlier part of the last century and the Africans in the diaspora that gave rise to new movements of emancipation and the reclaiming of dignity on the continent. Pan-Africanism as a movement, for example, was a result of the synergy released in the encounter between an oppressed people in the three worlds of Africa, the Caribbean islands and the Americas. The deconstruction of racial ideologies that accompanied the process made it possible for a people separated by deep seas and centuries of cultural mutilation to find in the void of separation the unique experiences that connected them to a larger vision of possibilities, i.e., the courage to hope! This courage was not just nurtured by "racial" or "ethnic" solidarity between those in the diaspora and on the continent but by an ethical vision of liberation from oppression.

However, the way the nation-state had matured in Europe did not ultimately reflect the original designs or ideologies of the pioneers of social change in Europe. Ceremonial monarchy still maintained a profound sense of prestige and domination that in some cases still undermined democracy. This is true especially in the case of Great Britain where by imperial decree unbridled expansion of the empire took place, as the reign of the British monarch until very recently was a fact of life in foreign territories. The incomplete overhaul of the feudal systems in Europe and the maturation of bourgeois modes of production and capital accumulation gave rise to forms of public democracy under the aegis of private control. Democracy became a system of mockery and a means by which class relations were maintained by giving the poor the tools of protest and the middle class the means to be rich.

The ethical defects in the coming into being of the modern nation-state in Europe were further aggravated by the fact that its transplantation into Africa was an abuse of the values and norms of her existence and that of her people. The horrifying events of genocide and massacres in Africa today can be traced and related to a pre-colonial design of the state and how juggling ethnic identities became the means for managing political clientelism and manipulating national resources at the behest of the colonial regime. The private and public spheres were then amalgamated by the colonial regime in an attempt to unify various nationalities (often called tribes) in order to control the access and use of natural resources and cheap human labour. It is known that French district officers, for example, never heeded bureaucratic procedures but exercised authority arbitrarily. Their British counterparts likewise practised a style of management known as indirect rule, a system of governance through remote control by proxy of a local traditional authority. In both cases, state bureaucracy was a personalized infrastructure delivering services for unquestioned loyalty of the subjects.

The colonial civil service, which Africans inherited, was essentially designed to channel imperial directives and provide administration of local goods and subjects; it cannot be viewed simply as the precursor to a modern bureaucratic system of delivery of goods and services. In some cases, the colonial administrators sat in local courts to dispense justice. For these practices, power needed to be centralized and personalized without clear differentiation of roles in governance.

The abuse and flouting of the rules of modern bureaucracy in the management of public affairs in Africa today can therefore be traced back to the culture of governance in colonial administration. This is not to say that African leadership is entirely hostage to that particular historical memory or game of domination. In fact, the leaders at the moment of legal independence became agents of "negative political inculturation" by appropriating the patrimonial values in African culture and introducing them into a migrated European imperial infrastructure of tyranny. While rejecting colonial domination, leaders welcomed its "civilizing" structures with new slogans of freedom but without justice. As a result, what was inherited and has been put to use is essentially an alien infrastructure that could properly be described as neither modern nor African.

It is even problematic to refer to the nation-state in Africa as a hybrid state that has assimilated both the European and African social political value systems. "Hybrid" would indicate a harmonized integration of both European and African value systems. It is more plausible to consider the post-colonial state in Africa as syncretistic in its struggle for identity. The constitutional regimes crafted at independence, for example, do not seem to reflect the authentic cultural infrastructures of communal autonomy in the rule of law and governance in the land. Instead, foundational documents were negotiated frameworks of power-sharing among the appointed elite and their clients. It is wrong to suggest that what Africa is going through today is an intrinsic reflection of the dilemmas and struggles of her ordinary population.

The problem is neither intrinsic nor entirely extrinsic. It is something in between that is in the process of self-definition. The struggles are rooted within communities of memory on the continent. The nation-state in Africa has largely remained the nexus of bureaucratization of power where "big men" and their clients negotiate the use and control of public resources. It does not have significance as a public entity of civil society that not only regulates but also sets the rules of delivery of public goods.

The dual crisis of the nation-state in Africa is deepened by the fact that it is also a victim of the ongoing trends of globalization. The process of globalization is causing internal weakening of the state's grip on critical dimensions of social and economic engagements. In the midst of a frustrated, diminishing role in development cooperation, new modes of tyranny have emerged. Some incumbent presidents employ every trick and manipulation to stay in office longer despite the constitutions and the wishes of their own people.

The post-colonial project of democracy in Africa which began in the wake of the new global political order of the late 1980s was essentially suffocated by the same factors that have only furthered the instability of the state. The disenfranchisement of the state in Africa by forces of globalization does not absolve African leaders from the crimes of internal tyranny and corruption. However, just as at independence in the 1960s when the partitioned Africa gained legal political autonomy from her colonial masters but retained the instruments of oppression, so it has been with the advent of multipartyism in the 1980s and 1990s.

The contemporary situation is but a replication of the colonial roots of power transfer and its complexities. The apparent relaxation of one-party political monopoly with the promises of Western-style democracy only occasioned the emergence of new clients in the same system of state tyranny. Multi-party elections became the panacea yet have not replaced political bargaining and vicious manipulations. Thus, the modern nation-state in Africa gained an international legitimacy in the family of nations globally, but not locally. These phenomena still pose the same dual dilemma of identity; i.e., the unsuccessful transplantation-construction of the European model of the colonial state, and the failure of ethical reconstruction of the nation-state as a public institution whose legitimacy is grounded on local aspirations. It is in the context of this state duality and within a dysfunctional system that corruption takes place.

5. The Crisis of Conscience

> The illusion of the sumptuous life made possible by profits from illicit practices has taken its toll on the very proponents of the new order.
>
> Thabo Mbeki, president of South Africa, in a speech at an anti-corruption conference, Cape Town

Corruption has been such a vital subject of analysis, especially with regard to Africa, that it has actually become a new sub-sector of social entrepreneurship for the middle class within organized civil society institutions in Africa. Unfortunately, while we address these issues with the good intention of finding solutions, numerous initiatives to combat corruption end up being sustained by the very peculiar systems that sustain egoistic interest and therefore avoid questions such as the widening gap between the rich and the poor. The problems of the workers increase as trade unions are gradually being compromised and more subtle ideologies of private investment, leading to corrupt practices, become more entrenched. In addressing the problem of corruption, we must never fall into the trap of becoming careerists who benefit from the plight of the victims of corruption. Today, there is a large body of literature dealing with the definitive nature and origin of corruption, albeit reflecting the various ideological schools of interpretation, especially where Africa is in question.

A growing awareness that corruption is a serious problem has galvanized support for an international and coordinated fight against it. In spite of this awareness, corruption remains a highly complex phenomenon. Conceptually, it is generally agreed that at the core of the problem lies some form of abuse of power. Such abuses of power or privilege are magnified by the transactional costs of corruption. At its heart may be the abuses of public office for direct or indirect personal gain. Indirect personal gain includes benefits that someone secures improperly for his or her organization (for example, a company, a political party or a non-profit organization).

Given the need for a common understanding of what is at stake and what kind of practices are to be eradicated, it is worthwhile to take a critical look at the approaches of anti-corruption organizations, most of which originate and are located in Europe and North America. Their empirical approach towards corrupt practices would tend to avoid value-bound conceptions and the more crucial historical facts, thereby enhancing consensus-building and allowing anti-corruption efforts to gain further momentum. Thus, various theories have been floated on the causes of corruption and its effects on development, and on measures to curb or control the growth of corruption.

While these debates have recently led to the formation of a variety of international watchdog institutions that provide updates and analysis on global trends, these institutions often function as satellite stations which monitor the activities of governments and state-related institutions in underdeveloped countries with regard to corrupt practices. They provide a wealth of information that influence and guide the policies of donor agencies and institutions in global financing which in turn serve the interest of the developed world. Most of them receive funding and support from the very governments and donor agencies in the North whose relationship with corresponding governments in the South is guided by factors of internal governance. Hence, possibilities of conflict of interest in their analysis are seldom discussed. That also explains why the subject of corruption has acquired such central appeal to global aid agencies and institutions in the North.

Enrique Dussel has spoken of the modern moment of nationhood as a complex combination of technology and conquest. According to Dussel, for the new world its reconstruction as "new" began in 1492 through encounter with a civilization that had the technological wherewithal to enforce its conception of universality on communities elsewhere. The modern moment is, in other words, a moment of conquest. Conquest is an unusual project. Its aim is to seize nothing but the land. The problem with such seizure, however, is that people often occupy land. Such occupation poses a moral problem, one that is usually resolved through an act of bad faith. The conquering people simply choose not to see that it is the people they are conquering, preferring instead to only see conquered lands. The land is treated as "peopleless". It is this form of denial that enabled the misrepresenting motif of Columbus's having "discovered" the Americas, and Jefferson simply having "purchased" much of North America west of the Mississippi from Napoleon Bonaparte.

Today, acts of displacement continue as borders are drawn and redrawn without recognition of populations who live on the land. In spite of the protectorates' jurisdictions, the complexity of protection has not always fared well in this regard. The scenario is classically Hobbesian: the sovereign can reign so long as it is able to protect those who live within its borders.

In modern political philosophy, the classic challenge to this view emerged in Jean-Jacques Rousseau's observation that sovereignty is also a matter of legitimacy, and protection alone is insufficient for legitimacy. A sovereign must be "right", which for Rousseau meant that it must work in the interest of human freedom (which he characterized as the "general will"), a notion that enables sovereignty to extend beyond its borders. Corruption involves a cultural construction of sovereignty in which even the public sphere beyond the boundaries is claimed as a colony by right.

Free market, politics and corruption

In this regard, the subject matter of corruption has gained a new, grand currency over the more urgent need to excavate hidden factors within structures and systems of capital accumulation that were infused at independence and are perpetrated by Western regimes in neo-colonial Africa. Most of the nascent nation-states in Africa pursue economic policies that are largely dictated by big business and international lending institutions, including budget cuts, privatization of basic utilities such as supply of water, telephone services, electricity, mass lay-off of workers in the public sector and the painful imposition of cost-sharing measures in health care even for the poor. Real power remains in the hands of those few who have the means of supply of goods and resources including multinational companies which determine the future of millions of Africans. In this order, relationships can be defined only in terms of aggression and submission. This reduces any form of participation, including democracy, to a mockery of a mere counting of votes every five years. The episodic dimensions of democratic practice become the central focus of interventions, not the sustainable participation of local communities in issues and interests pertaining to their own destiny.

One cannot therefore honestly face the problem of corruption without a clear comprehension of the connections between the politics of resource management and distribution at the international level and national class relations. These are often interwoven and sometimes even camouflaged by the contemporary ideologies of the market. We know all too well that markets (*sokoni* = Swahili for "at the market-place") have always been a socio-economic reality in Africa, and so what I refer to here has to do more with the conditions (ideological and otherwise) under which free-market operations take place, and how these conditions are intrinsic to the nature of corruption.

We do not ignore or discount the empirical evidence that corruption in its crude manifestation is very much alive in public life, now that local leaders in both political and civil society institutions are largely responsible as collaborators in a rotten system, especially in the direct, massive looting and misappropriation of national resources. Much research being done to determine the causes of bureaucratic corruption in Africa by Western scholars indicates that African civil servants may be obliged to share the proceeds of their public offices with their kinfolk. The African extended family is also to be blamed for exerting pressure on the civil servants (read aspiring lower middle class) by forcing them to engage in corrupt practices of nepotism. Bureaucrats themselves are believed to exploit their public positions to generate benefits for themselves, their families, and their ethnic or social connections. Thus, in studying corruption in Africa, researchers have tended to place emphasis on the structural and individual conditions that may contribute to corrupt behaviour, without making clear distinctions between what was essentially a social safety-net system (based on the values of particular cultural societies in Africa) and the responses to the problems of capital accumulation that threaten the survival of neighbourhood communities. It is generally accepted as a given fact in most of the scholarship and research that, due to the absence of strong civil society structures, there is general lack of dedication to the public good.

It was even suggested in the headline and articles of *The Economist* of 13-19 May 2000 that Africans are inherently passive and prefer to be comfortable under the tyranny of a corrupt local leadership. It is also said that, because in many of these African countries civil service employees view public service as an opportunity for self-enrichment, another open project of re-colonization may be the only answer to the woes of Africa. This kind of analysis does not even pretend to be sophisticated in its attempt to construct a framework of racial reasoning on the issue of corruption. It relies heavily on popular perceptions of Africa as disseminated by the Western media. Yet, interestingly enough, these backward notions are held by many, including some African scholars.

We must seek to address the ways in which the predominant regimes of capital accumulation under the aegis of colonial governance were largely responsible for the new (un)ethic (or should we say mode of a legislated but corrupt form of governance) by which corruption became a way of life in Africa. In the context of globalization, the colonial factors are further aggravated by a complex system of delivery of goods corresponding to the appetites produced by images of the good life supplied by advertisement. The illusion of an infinite supply of the good life through mechanisms of production and distribution is driven by the ethic of competition which rewards the rich and punishes the poor for being poor.

Underlying the problem of corruption is access to public goods as if they were private commodities. The lack of distinction between what is essentially public and what is private does not exist exclusively in the "bloated conscience" or minds of corrupt individuals, but is the product of structures supported by ideologies of self-regulating market mechanisms. The power of so-called market forces over public sovereignty is the key to understanding the environment in which corruption is taking place in Africa.

One cannot separate social goals from either personal or community goods. The absence of the distinction and preservation of public goods as being under the custody of the community is in essence the deliberate undertaking of neoliberalism.

A brutal system of exclusion gradually has led to the destruction of inherent social capital derived from the communitarian ethic of life originally found among communities in Africa. The consequence of this is the prevailing culture of nihilism and social death. The new ethic of "the good life" (nurtured by deification of hedonistic values) which destroys the moral fabric of life-giving and sustaining relationships (within the human community, the cosmos and the spirits) is death-driven. Mere situational and empirical analysis of the problems of corruption as they relate to colonial rule is not enough. One must go deeper into the roots of the ethos of colonial adventures, slavery and trading of slaves and the subsequent rise of local tyrants who still reign in Africa with the tools and ideas of the colonial master. Corruption is an intrinsic part of this whole system that benefits the rich and robs not only the poor but creation itself of its goodness and integrity. It is from this perspective that I seek to ponder on the alternatives for Africa.

Colonial roots of corruption

While synonymous with particular acts of bribery, the essence of corruption encompasses the appropriation and misuse of authority by alien institutions and individuals. As in the case of colonialism, corruption is driven by the crude hedonistic tendencies of capital accumulation favouring the interests of a particular people or race. Thus in colonialism (apart from the obvious economic factors) both political and social systems were introduced for the purpose of rewarding or punishing selected groups in the society depending on their respective utility to the colonization process. These systems provided the initial socio-economic framework through which local and public resources were looted and diverted for non-public use to the exclusive profit of particular communities or groups of social agents. The establishment of colonialism itself was an act of corruption.

The catalytic influence was that of King Leopold II of the Belgians, who had spent twenty years in the search for a tropical colony when at last he found in the Congo basin, as revealed by the explorations of H.M. Stanley, a goal worthy of his desires. Knowing that Belgium did not share his expansionist dreams, he made his approach under cover of an international organization which turned itself gradually into the Congo Independent State, in which form it existed from 1885 until 1908 when Belgium finally assumed responsibility. Already by about 1878, Leopold's preparatory moves were beginning to attract the attention of would-be imitators. Colonial pressure groups were founded in both France and Germany, and expeditions were dispatched to obtain treaties with African rulers in areas considered suitable for future colonies.

Meanwhile, in 1881, France declared a protectorate over Tunis, and in 1882 army officers in Egypt organized a coup d'état against the Khedive's government as protest against the economies imposed by the country's European creditors. Britain and France agreed to act together to quell the revolt by a temporary military occupation. At the last minute, the French withdrew from the projected expedition for reasons of internal politics, so that Britain occupied Egypt alone, thereby greatly stimulating the acquisitive fever developing in the rest of Europe.

It was in these circumstances that the German chancellor Bismarck called a conference of the European powers, which met in Berlin from December 1884 until April 1885, to discuss the future of western Africa. Ostensibly, the purpose was to restrain expansionism rather than to encourage it.

In King Leopold's Congo, the population living between the estuary and Lake Malebo were impressed into labour by military means for portage and road-building, while the army, the *force publique*, was built up by purchases of "freed slaves" from the Swahili Arab traders of the Ituri Forest and the Lomami. These recruits were taken a thousand miles from their homes for training, and then engaged for seven to nine years under the rules of martial law. By 1900, their numbers had grown to nearly 20,000, and it was these men, later posted as gendarmes in almost every village of the forested areas, who were used to compel the unfortunate inhabitants to go out and tap the wild landolphia rubber vines, often to the neglect of their own food plantations. "The more gendarmes, the more rubber," as the saying went. The best that can be said is that the period of outrageous exploitation was a short one, lasting from about 1898 till about 1905. While it endured, the boom in "red rubber" saved King Leopold from otherwise certain bankruptcy.

The intervening imperial powers had to corrupt some members and leaders in local communities in order to infiltrate the African hinterland and establish the infrastructure for "divide and rule". The ethos of colonial governance (i.e., indirect rule by proxy) is largely responsible for creating powerful leaders and institutions with neither the consent nor the participation of the peoples' conscience. The fact that the colonial administration itself was alien to the people meant that the people did not have any allegiance to it, and neither did they feel obliged to be committed to it. So they hated it and whenever possible sought to undermine it. Even when it became evident that the colonies would be granted independence, the colonial regimes quickly developed reform programmes that would enable the full participation of the indigenous peoples to address the fundamental issues related to self-governance. Most of the constitutional rules that were adopted by African countries at legal independence were crafted overseas in the interests of the indigenous peoples represented by urban elites, most of whom had been educated in Europe and had accepted Western political norms of governance and economic systems.

In addition to the fact that these urban elites were Westernized, not in touch with the conditions in the rural sectors of their respective countries, and had long been away from their rural homes, they usually had objectives and interests that were significantly different from those of peasant communities. Constitutional documents adopted at the Lancaster conference, for example, were alien and did not seriously consider the aspirations, desires and needs of the rural populations. The people were neither enfranchized nor were they provided with the facilities to participate effectively in the selection of the rulers. Thus constitutional rules of statecraft led to the production of leviathan states whose powers were then used by political coalitions under international neo-colonial hegemony to amass wealth for a few individuals and cartels while the rest of the people languished in poverty.

Colonial rule introduced a governance paradigm devoid of any ethical or just considerations towards the people being governed. By virtue of the fact that the people were subjects and not citizens, they did not feel any obligation to respect, trust or obey the colonial government. This means that there were two parallel systems existing side by side: one alien and oppressive and expressed through public life; the other indigenous, life-fulfilling, liberating and expressed through community life. Corruption was the intrinsic nature in the former while, in the latter, corruption was virtually non-existent and when it appeared was dealt with ruthlessly. At independence, the road not taken was the one that could have led to the recovery of the African heritage in which just and participatory governance would have been at the centre of community life.

The hand-picking of rulers (whether military or civilian) by any of the superpowers reinforced rather than corrected the colonial rule. During the cold war, corruption became institutionalized at the behest of both Western and Eastern hegemony. The *realpolitik* factors of global power arrangements suffocated local initiatives for emancipation and allowed room for the emergence of tyrants who used the very instruments of colonial statecraft against the people.

In the final analysis, corruption was really a conspiracy between the foreign powers and their local collaborators. In time, it has become malignant, spreading out to consume the moral and social fabric of the society.

As we have demonstrated in the preceding chapter, the nation-state in Africa is a very recent phenomenon alienated from the social and political memory of grassroots communities in rural Africa. The nation-state in its current form is therefore perceived by most of these communities as an impostor. The means by which it comes into being is frustrating to the aspirations and dreams of local communities and civil society.

Corruption and development

It is interesting to note that contemporary theories of political development in Africa continue to focus on corruption as the major impediment to modernization of the nation-states in Africa. These theories are developed without any criticism of the models of the nation-state form itself which is not only facing a critical historical moment but certainly undergoing gradual but radical change in Europe.

Since the early 1960s, significant research and studies on the nature and origin of corruption have been focused on public sector conduct and the question of leadership. These are symptomatic dimensions of the problem and hence the unresolved prescriptive measures hinge upon clean-up operations as policed by international financial institutions such as IMF and the World Bank – themselves part of the problem rather than the solution.

Most of the recent documents that define and discuss the "the African predicament" take the lenses of neo-liberalism as the basic instruments of understanding social reality and arrive at the wrong prescriptions to public sector corruption in Africa. Corruption is defined broadly as the misuse or abuse of public resources for private or sectarian interests. The so-called modern distinctions between the private and public realms with regard to functions of the state are blurred by lack of ideological clarity regarding the boundaries of the public and private spheres vis-a-vis the state.

It has been assumed that, at its core, the modernized nation-state enjoys a stable, autonomous, professional civil service. As an institution, the civil service is supposed to function with corporate efficiency to ensure proper administration and delivery of public goods. Thus, payment of salaries to the civil service must be seen to be commensurate with public responsibilities, and promotion must be based on merit. But in the case of most African countries, where the autonomy of the civil service is absent due to the residues of the colonial state and where public space is overwhelmingly politicized, it has been largely impossible to apply European models of corporate efficiency.

The ethical basis for the existence of the state as a public institution in its current form must now be questioned, even though we do not seem to have the vocabulary for alternative social thought relevant to the future of our people. We all know that, in terms of direct corruption, there are individuals within particular states who seem to have unlimited access to or control of certain public resources who do not see anything wrong in turning public matters into private use. Consequently, while the debate continues, public resources diminish and the public sector is weakened due to privatization or individualization of state resources.

During the cold war, the state in Africa under the siege of bipolar power contests became increasingly a private institution. When the state becomes a private corporate enterprise, then surely even the so-called second liberation movements among a disenfranchised middle class will fail to claim the energies of the silent poor who live under the yoke of dual oppression. Reclaiming the state is the necessary means of addressing the problem of corruption. This requires the widening of public space through participation of the poor in public policy formulation. The phenomenon of the private state is essentially the heart of corruption. It results in poor public policy and generates a multitude of problems ranging from incompetence of public delivery systems, ignorance and, at the end of the spectrum, poverty. So the cancer of corruption in Africa with its origin and sustenance in colonial factors is directly linked to the problem of local leadership because, as the state gradually falls into the private hands of whoever is heading its public structures, accountability and transparency are undermined.

Why is it that even countries that have continued to adapt to the rules and systems of democracy in order to enhance the legitimacy and authority of the people over the state in Africa do not seem to reap the expected fruits of development as anticipated by those seeking to reform and modernize the state in its current form? The most dangerous situation is a quasi-democratic state where the process of democratization itself legitimates local corrupt practices as in the case of Kenya, or tyranny over the majority as in the case of Zimbabwe.

We need to re-examine corruption clean-up strategies for Africa proposed by international monetary institutions and seek to show why they have been ineffective. African countries, like many other developing countries, have tried several strategies in an effort to minimize levels of bureaucratic corruption and appease donor agencies in order to comply with impossible conditions of aid. These include responses to societal, legal, market and political strategies that are based on the global economies of the West. Corruption has been reinforced by "aid" which in some cases was outright bribery paid to prop up dictators. In some instances today, further aid amid adverse economic situations has led to the survival of local tyrants.

All approaches to corruption clean-up represent the manipulation of outcomes within a given set of rules and presuppose the existence of efficient counteracting institutions. The evidence shows, however, that most judiciary systems and police forces in African countries are not properly constrained by the law and that many civil servants (including judges and police officers) are themselves corrupt. As a result, most clean-up programmes in Africa have been unsuccessful.

Alternative ethics of governance

The link between economic growth and state politics in Africa is largely made without a keen interest in the origins of the nation-state as a colonial instrument. We must always remember that the contemporary struggle is an attempt to survive in the context of globalization. That is why the statistics of economic growth in Africa are not only disappointing but, coupled with the recent AIDS epidemic, border on the catastrophic.

In Tanzania during the regime of its first president, Mwlimu Julius Nyerere, the Leaders' Code of Conduct encompassed the integrity of the impeccable Nyerere and aimed to comprehend the symbiosis between public office and private interests. The success of the late Nyerere against corruption may largely be attributed to his effective attempt at crafting an alternative public ethic of governance that affirmed the values and culture of his people. However, one historical figure alone cannot be held accountable for two entire generations of people struggling with the vestiges of colonial rule. The focus must go beyond the integrity of the leader to building alternative institutions of governance that are anchored on the values and common vision of the people. Corruption must be seen as generic to systems and structures of capital accumulation which do not derive their legitimacy from the local institutions of governance and values.

Even as effective clean-up programmes are designed, results of attempts at structural reforms seem to be elusive because links to the colonial past are still very strong. Bureaucratic forms of corruption are taking a toll due to the fact that people in civil service are generally responsible for the stability of the state and hence seek compensation and favours through informal means by either direct manipulation of the political system or outright bribery. The three arms of government (executive, legislative and judiciary) are usually held together by the executive branch which in turn ensures the stability of other sectors of government. However, the state's internal stability is often guaranteed by institutions outside the formal state. The military and related security forces provide necessary structures of stability, so their compensation comes outside the formal channels. Arms dealers are usually middle persons and, like estate agents, work on a commission basis. So it is of no surprise that they often sell the most expensive goods at the highest possible price to their customers, whether or not the goods fit their client's requirements. Huge silent kick-backs change hands in the process leading up to the selection of primary bidders. The deals include modern fighter jets, helicopters, fire-arms and even equipment such as tanks and riot gear to quell local unrest. Ironically, these deals are often made by former colonial masters such as the UK, Germany, France, and even the USA.

Thus, excess capital is required by those in power to stay in power and ascertain the trust and absolute loyalty of all the apparatus of the state. This apparatus, in turn, comes to be included in the society of invisible government that actually runs the government. Informal political agents who influence key cultural groups are also to be compensated because through them the state monitors the activities of autonomous communities and societies. Other individuals, institutions and interest groups also seek favours from the state in relationships of patronage.

Political coalitions in certain countries emerge in times of crisis, seeking ways to subvert the existing rules to redistribute national income and wealth in their favour, sometimes even under the guise of democracy. This trend is more pervasive in countries that do not have clear, efficient, self-regulating constitutional regimes that are outside the sphere of influence of those in power. The rules guiding relations between those who are custodians of public resources and those who facilitate the redistribution and management of such resources are often vague and subject to manipulation. So a culture of secrecy prevails not just within the local polity but also with respect to international transactions.

Corruption is a global phenomenon. Much has been written about it in other parts of the South. The Western media and social analysts have been covering high-level corruption in Asia and Latin America. Organizations and individuals involved in "corruption watch" on countries of the South have increased their vigilance over the years. Due to advanced information technology their findings are up to date and circulate widely in all parts of the world. It has been alleged that corruption played no small part in the collapse of the political regimes of Marcos of Philippines, Suharto of Indonesia and Fujimori of Peru, to name but a few. In big business, corruption has contributed to the economic and social destabilization of many countries in those regions. Much has also been written about corruption being endemic in the collapsed communist regimes of Eastern Europe. Corruption was, arguably, a significant factor in the demise of communism in Eastern Europe. It corroded the social fabric of society and crippled the ethical base of the system. Thus, corruption in the higher echelons of power in those regimes provided an added reason for the capitalist West to discredit communism as polity.

Corruption in the West and the North

Comparatively, a great deal less has been written about corruption in the advanced capitalist societies in Western Europe and North America. The Watergate scandal of 1972 was a window into the sophisticated methods of corruption in the way political affairs are run in the rich industrialized West. Watergate even came to attain global usage as a generic term to define big-time corrupt practices. President Nixon was not the last casualty of Watergate. Since then, corruption has been the cause of political casualties in European politics. The adage "politics is a dirty game" (itself coined not in developing countries but in Europe) still holds true in the much-vaunted "accountable" and "clean" governance of the NATO region.

Whether we consider the poor countries of the South or the rich countries of the North, *realpolitik* is the name of the game whose common denominator is greed for power. But as is becoming evident, greed is endemic in the business world of the advanced capitalist society. In the media there are ample revelations to suggest that, beneath the veneer of efficiency and entrepreneurial assertiveness, there is to be found some of the ugliest corrupt practices in the world. Insatiable corporate greed is likely to have a huge economic, social and ethical toll on US society. Considering that the USA is the strongest economy in the world, the dire economic consequences are bound to be felt globally.

Initially, financial reports in 2002 talked of corporate scandals, corporate wrongdoing and irresponsible practices of a few corporate executives. But corruption by any other name is still corruption. With the revelations that WorldCom had overstated a key measure of earnings by more than $3.8 billion over five quarters dating back to January 2001 (see *Time*, 8 July 2002), corruption is now being cited throughout the media to describe the malpractice of big corporations in the USA. Judging by the number of big corporations under investigation for their accounting practices or whose book-keeping records have raised concerns, it becomes clear that what is at stake is not just a one-off incident but a pattern of deception and behaviour practised in the world of unbridled capitalism. It appears that greed and deception are intrinsic to the system. Mike Oxley of the US House Financial Services Committee says that "it looks like good old-fashioned fraud".

A lot is left to be desired as far as the ethical integrity of American corporations is concerned. In his analysis, Daniel Kadlec points out that "the plunge in WorldCom shares has cost investors upwards of $175 billion – nearly three times what was lost in the implosion of Enron. WorldCom is not yet financially bankrupt, but it's clear that it – like a fat slice of corporate America – has been ethically bankrupt for years." As a result of these revelations, confidence and trust in the leadership of corporate America has been waning fast. Over two-thirds of Americans are said to have less trust in the management of publicly traded companies, and up to 75 percent have little faith in the integrity of financial statements.

What effect all this will have on the American economy in general is yet to be fully determined. What is evident by mid-2003 is that, besides the financial losses to the investors, thousands of jobs have been lost. Enron alone has laid off 12,600 and WorldCom was said to have eliminated 16,000 jobs immediately, with more to follow. With some of the corporations expected to file bankruptcy, thousands more jobs are at stake with all the social consequences to the victims, their families and communities. Because of partnerships, mutual funds, financial service, investment interests and the sheer pervasiveness of global capitalism, many more corporations in the USA and elsewhere in the world are likely to be linked with the discredited American corporations in one way or another. Already a number of other firms have been exposed because of their dealings with WorldCom.

Corporate Watergate is not limited to American firms. European companies are known to have been involved in corrupt practices, especially in million-dollar development projects in developing countries. This invariably involved collaboration with senior civil servants and politicians in the respective countries. Dam projects, supply of heavy-duty equipment, road and bridge construction have been among the popular candidates in this respect. Very often, the projects are carried out by consortia.

A classic example is a dam project in Lesotho which has been a subject of judicial investigation in the last two years. The investigation was initiated by the government of Lesotho with little or no support at all from the home governments of the European and other rich countries whose companies were involved. Other institutions like the World Bank were discouraging spectators to the investigative process. The judge's findings are (according to the *Guardian Weekly* of 11-17 July 2002) "a damning account of the way the giant British engineering firm Balfour Betty paid bribes into a Swiss bank account to get construction contracts" for the Lesotho dam project. The case involved the transfer of £123,310 into a Zurich bank account which was controlled by a French agent. The amount would eventually be drawn in favour of the Lesotho chief executive of the dam project, but not before a generous commission had been taken by the

French agent and other associated intermediaries. Worse still, the "bribe cash was profitably lodged to earn interest in the Channel Islands. Swiss records reveal at least one deposit of £63,000 at the UBS branch of St Helier, Jersey, and another of £115,452 (£75,000) at the Jersey branch of the Union Banque Privée." When he released his findings, the judge in Lesotho stressed that the companies and agencies involved had deliberately entered into a corrupt agreement because "they must have known the payments to the Swiss banks involved bribery".

From the above, we can draw the conclusion that corruption in the rich industrialized countries is commonly practised at the macro level. It is sophisticated and involves millions and even billions of dollars. In the poor developing countries of Africa, corruption is practised primarily at a micro level, sometimes for purposes of economic survival.

But big-time corruption is becoming more common in Africa, as well. Those involved are well-placed civil servants and politicians who seem to be learning the ropes from their counterparts in Europe and North America. They are at the stage which is described by the Russian *nouveaux riches* as initial accumulation of capital. Once they are in fact rich, they may stop the crude methods of corruption and adopt the more refined corrupt practices that characterize the corporate business world in the advanced capitalist economies. While it is clear that corruption is practised globally, it is also clear that in a society where corruption is accepted as a norm for behaviour, that society will hardly progress in anything. Sadly, this is the case with many countries in Africa.

Networks of corruption

Corruption in Africa often involves participation by foreign entities, including major corporations and individuals seeking contracts and business opportunities, especially now in the era of liberalization in which state and public resources are on sale in the name of privatization. Liberalization itself provides the space and opportunity for the survival of a rogue state through reinvention of the same structures but with new strategic alliances. These are built-in cooperation with the same old but recycled civil service bureaucracies, and hence the corruption "feeding chain" continues, albeit in less visible channels.

Thus, activities include payment of bribes to obtain import and export licences, foreign exchange permits, and investment and production licences. To minimize costs imposed on their enterprises by the state, owners of capital may bribe civil servants and other members of the enforcement community in order to receive favourable tax treatment. Civil servants are also able to extort bribes from individuals and groups seeking access to government-subsidized goods and services. The resources expended by entrepreneurs on bribes represent an illegal tax on economic activity and may be viewed as an attenuation of property rights.

In many African countries, rulers do not seem to be genuinely interested in effective clean-up programmes because corruption represents an important source of revenue and a means through which rulers channel resources to supporters. Corruption nurtures the tricks of the tyrant, offers the capital for survival by not only protecting the interests of the colonial regime but also nurturing a "safety net" against any social discontent, thereby maintaining "peace and stability".

Consider import and export procedures currently in place due to liberalization and introduction of more sophisticated, efficient delivery systems in my own country, Kenya. It is conceivable that many of the layers of bureaucracy in processing relevant information could be cut out due to the use of high-technology techniques. For example, an electronic data interchange system would cut out the messengers who carry files from office to office and who use their access as levers for demanding *kitu kidogo!* (i.e., something small). One is likely to hear comments through the corridors of such offices that in order to be successful in import/export you have to be corrupt since *mkono mtupu haulambwi* (no one licks an empty palm) while bidding for a government contract.

With such cultural jargon, unscrupulous agents (who are also victims of the corruption of the state) twist the sayings of the wise in Africa and take advantage of a rotten system, transforming what it is into a norm of survival in a capitalist system. Consider a situation where for an office messenger to move a file from point A to point B one must grease his/her palm. Those that fail to do so have their document delayed/hidden or even lost in the process. In the latter case, they have to start all over again, a much more costly exercise than the original "palm-greasing" would have been. What is the overall effect of these corruption practices? An obvious one is the slowing down of activities, and the creation of an informal bureaucracy that runs parallel to that of government. This kind of corruption of "oiling the hands" of the middle persons is to be understood as an alternative means of self-initiated compensation by a frustrated and disenfranchised working poor. Persons engaged in such practices often take home a salary that is usually not more than $50 a month!

In this way, labour-wage relationships are distorted and undermining the state becomes a lucrative industry in itself. Morale and work ethic slowly die away because merit for good or hard work is replaced by the quick fix and shortcuts offered by corruption. All one needs is strategic placement in a spot where one wields power and has easy access to the instruments of delivery and control of public resources.

One of the main questions in combating corruption is how to institute public disclosure of assets by public servants and politicians. Good governance demands high standards of personal integrity and discipline of public officers, in particular among politicians, i.e., the president, government ministers and their deputies. It is imperative that the public be aware of the income of public officials and politicians. There must be registry of assets, regularly filled in, and a monitoring mechanism by independent anti-corruption commissions with powers to enforce policy and procedures to protect public assets.

The Zambian parliamentary and ministerial code of conduct act of 1999, for example, prohibits any minister, deputy minister or member of parliament from dishonesty or improperly acquiring any pecuniary advantage or assisting in the acquisition of pecuniary advantage by another person. It prohibits improper use of or benefit from information which is obtained in the course of their official duties and which is not generally available to the public; the disclosure of any official information to unauthorized persons; exertion of any improper influence in the appointment, promotion, discipline or removal of a public officer; direct or indirect conversion of government property for personal or any other use than that stipulated; the soliciting of or acceptance of transfers of economic benefits other than benefits of nominal value including customary hospitality and token gifts; gifts from close family members; or transfers pursuant to an enforceable property right of the member or pursuant to a contract for which full value is given. Progressive as the Zambian act is on paper, in reality it fails to standardize the declaration format making it impossible to compare and measure submissions of assets, their movement and acquisition over a specific period. Excessive gifts, especially when frequently given, raise suspicion. There must be a system of discernment, codification and enforcement of legislation against corruption.

Public officials must declare all their assets, liabilities and interests on a regular basis. It is not sufficient to declare assets at the start and end of one's tenure of service. This is because assets and liabilities can fluctuate, and one may acquire a new business interest at any time. The record should show the pattern of an individual's assets and liabilities. There must be a system in place whereby the government can track fluctuations of public servants' assets.

An ombudsman whose office is independent may be more ideal than anti-corruption commissions like the one experimented with, for example, in Kenya. It should carry out impartial investigations on matters of corruption even if suspicion falls on the highest office in the land. It is by instituting such a mechanism that it will be possible to redress the kind of situation where ordinary people, especially the small-scale farmers, artisans and fishermen, work very hard to earn a living, and others hardly do any proportional work to earn more. It is sad to note that even those charged with administering soft loans in cooperative societies demand to be bribed before approving a straightforward loan application.

Corrupt practices of this kind reveal that what we are dealing with is not just an unfair mode of transaction that hurts the economy but a sick system which in the end hurts the poor and punishes those who choose to live with integrity. Broadly speaking, when state enterprise is in the hands of powerful private institutions that dictate the rules of ownership, what you have is a people who surrender and even trade their sovereignty to the willing buyer.

What is emerging is a scenario in which, on the one hand, local investors happily collude with corrupt governments or public officials to escape legal demands for accountability. On the other hand, global investors are more interested in quick, huge transactions through direct personal relations with actors within state institutions. Preferential bidding for state contracts and favours in the acquisition of assets in the newly liberalized public sectors such as those of telecommunication, energy and water distribution are some of the most coveted targets.

The level of people's participation in governance and distribution of public resources is instrumental in the reduction and possible alleviation of certain forms of corruption. Virtually every discourse on the subject of corruption sees a close tie to poor participation in governance. Once the state is in the hands of private individuals with uncontrolled power, the inevitable tendency is to misuse their authority to such ends as to justify calling the situation one of corruption.

But flawed governance is not just the outcome of a lack of certain systems of efficiency, as claimed in the maxims of corporate ethics. Rather, it is deeply rooted in the history of consciousness and values of the "other" that unfortunately has become part of Africa's social reality. Unless we discover an alternative vision of our being in the world as dignified participants, in the making of history, based upon a new notion of the good life that appreciates and affirms our heritage, we are doomed to be victims of corruption. Neither the excessive regulation of community resources nor the privatization of public space is a solution to the problem of corruption. For the cause of corruption would remain deeply rooted in colonial history.

We shall uproot corruption through a new understanding of the dignity of who we are, as well as through radical movements of ethical consciousness that infiltrate all levels of participation in governance to guide our future actions and attitudes. Such movements need not be political, nor a part of organized sectors within civil society. Yet while exercising their autonomy outside the state, they ought to possess the means to make demands and seek concessions from the state.

In other words, it is only through a mobilized and sustained grassroots resistance to the tyranny of the state, and the emergence of sites of autonomy in which ordinary citizens may reclaim their dignity and proclaim their civility, that the instruments and legacy of corruption will be destroyed in the continent. The role of the church in this process could be invaluable, given its vast social capital and accessibility to the ordinary people in the community. In a society where money becomes the currency of dignity, corrupt power arrangements will definitely lead to institutional paralysis. It is this paralysis that has led to a crisis that is ultimately neither political nor merely economic in Africa, but a crisis of the spirit.

6. Human Dignity and Modernity in Africa

> For Europe, for ourselves and for humanity, comrades, we must turn over a new leaf, we must work out new concepts, and try to set afoot a new man.
>
> Frantz Fanon, *The Wretched of the Earth*, p.316

The question of human dignity has remained the central underlying theme of this publication. We shall now venture directly into the sphere of influence and confluence of the forces of modernity and the question of retention or rejection of the dignity of the African people.

We cannot escape the problem of situating modernity in the African context without first coming to grips with the internal contradictions within the notion of modernity. The dawn of modernity is mostly traced by political commentators through the development of the nation-state and the application of certain types of technology associated with particular scientific innovations in recent times.

However, there are profound ideological undergirdings in the understanding of the meaning of modernity itself. The ideological bases of modernity tend to depend on particular contexts or world-views. We shall proceed to work with the historical assumption that the reality of modernity is not mono-causal, but rather that there are a multiplicity of identities which comprise African modernity. In the early 1960s, as earlier discussed, the euphoria of independence covered the whole of Africa. The fervour of nationalism and enthusiasm for change made that period the ideological crucible for modern Africa. After Ghana's independence in 1957, the wave of independence moved from the west coast over central Africa to the east and then to southern Africa. The dark continent, the land of burnt faces, as it was once described, had proved its own dignity in view of an increasingly unfriendly world.

While Africa was slowly emerging from the enclave of oppression, something interesting was taking place in Europe. This time, it was not the Berlin conference, but the Berlin wall that had divided the European world into East and West, communist and capitalist. This division of the world would now further divide Africa even more comprehensively. It was no longer based only on European economic interests, but on American and Russian ideological interests. Africa's helplessness no longer lay in the hands of the French or the British, but in the hands of Americans and Soviets and their allies in Europe and the rest of the world.

In this way, many African states became involved in new global power struggles soon after their independence. The United States had the advantage that the former colonialists were her allies. The USA demonstrated her political power through economic and military means, and US political leaders consistently repeated that "in every cooperation with the rest of the world, American business interests come first". During the cold-war era, American economic interests in Africa were coupled with US geo-political hegemonic interests which spared little effort to check any expansion of communism on the continent. As the Soviets found more and more followers in central and southern Africa through supporting liberation struggles there, the American military presence in Africa intensified.

America sought to make allies out of those African leaders who were obviously impressed by Western capitalism. Personalities like Kamuzu Banda in Malawi, Jomo Kenyatta in Kenya and Mobutu Sese Seko in Zaire gave in to the American strategy owing to the guaranteed stability that was offered against a possible communist infiltration. African governments paid enormous attention to security matters and increased military spending at the expense of economic development.

The Soviets got involved with local political leaders who sought an alternative base for fighting neo-colonialism. They knew well that the deep discontent of African states with their former colonial masters provided a perfect opportunity to popularize communism among the local people. African leaders who appeared radical and seemed to be searching for new paradigms were, therefore, approached. Among them were Kwame Nkrumah in Ghana, Modibo Keita in Mali,

Gamal Abdel Nasser in Egypt, Ben Bella in Algeria and Patrice Lumumba in Congo.

In this way, Africa became a territory disputed by both super-powers soon after independence. The arms race during the cold war resulted in the expansion of militaries in Africa, which led in turn to forty-seven senseless wars and increased internal instability in most African countries. Millions of people lost their lives, and many more millions fled or are still fleeing today. Africa is rightly referred to as "the continent of refugees".

The quest to recover, reclaim and restore the dignity of the African peoples should constitute one of the biggest challenges in the 21st century. The essence of the African vocation is the restoration of human dignity. The suffering and misery experienced in Africa today is an invitation to awaken in the hearts and minds of her people the possibility of a new life that is rich and fulfilling. If her people are made aware of the alternatives, Africa shall not endure in the solitude of misery, neither shall she be eternally banished without hope. The listening spirit will enable Africa to discern messages of hope even through walls of hopelessness. This spirit will direct the people towards a new vision of life that can purify the past and bring new life to the enslaving forms of global migrant institutions.

By standing against solutions to her problems imposed from outside, Africa will affirm her fresh look at the world as the means to restoration of a healthy, unifying vision and of dignity to her people. In this chapter, I want to revisit the authentic struggles in Africa to regain her humanity, struggles that have taken place amid the contradictions of the conditions prevalent in this era of globalization.

From the point of view of the Christian faith, the foundation of human dignity lies in the fact that each person is created in the image of God. Each person, irrespective of sex, status, social station, race or creed, bears the divine stamp that reads "created in the image of God" *(imago Dei)*. The dignity of every person is therefore inviolable because its authenticity comes from none other than the Creator. All human rights flow from the recognition and affirmation of the dignity of the individual person.

Thus, as we leave the lengthy period of human-rights activism – when the conventional language of rights has been preoccupied with the notions of freedom and liberty in the spirit of the Enlightenment – the dignity of the human person as *imago Dei* must become our point of departure. Dignity is not an empirical result of philosophies of human autonomy produced during the Enlightenment but the human reality of the *imago Dei*. In addition, as in the African traditional point of view, the individuality (not to be confused with possessive individualism) of a person, as created by God, is what matters most and gives value to our relations with others.

The person's dignity and worth is not, therefore, derived from level of education, position or material wealth. Rather, to be is to be in right relationship with other human beings, the rest of the creation and the Creator. It is important that we lay the ethical foundation of human identity in our discourse regarding human dignity. For the African people, the relational dimension is accorded the highest value in measuring the quality of life in the community and the society at large. This relational dimension was greatly undermined and compromised by slavery and colonialism, and it needs to be recovered and reconstructed. It is enriched by the abundance of life. We who live in the Western world are often trapped in the dilemma of choice posed by the human need for community and an environment that is hostile to the values of community. But human dignity does not arise in the context of market forces; rather, it is part of the communitarian network of life.

The communitarian ethic

The communitarian ethic of the inter-relatedness of life as a gift of creation is at the heart of Africa's contribution to modern civilization. In most of the African belief and value systems, all human beings subsist in a moral universe. It is a universe sustained by a web of relationships connecting the distant past, mediated by the present, as the future happens.

The moral culture of palaver and story-telling is the means by which the past becomes verbalized in the present, giving value to daily experiences of life through memories of days long gone by. We need to reconstruct the essential elements that contribute to the nurturing of a communitarian ethic. These include an integrity of wholeness – whole person, whole life, whole relations within the whole community. This challenges us to move from our alienated state to a state of wholeness and reconciliation, to move from alienation in regard to one's culture and community to wholeness.

The second element denotes being in, and belonging to, the community. All members are obliged to share and contribute to the growth of life of the whole community. To guard the common welfare of the community is the responsibility, first of all, of the community leaders. Yet, the people as a whole are co-responsible because the capacity of the leaders essentially depends on every single community member. Between the leaders and single members, there exists a dialectical relationship. The academics in the community are challenged to be active members in the life of the community, allowing their intellectual resources to interact constructively with real situations on the ground. African intellectuals must strive to be organic intellectuals fully integrated into the life of the community and putting their gifts and talents at the disposal of the community. That way, the intellectuals, civic leaders and community members reinforce one another through the whole body, the community.

The third element is cultural renaissance, which is a vital element to the recovery of the dignity of the African peoples. In the African world, everything can be brought back to the concept of life. An important dimension in this vein is the reconstruction of religious values that ensure abundant life for all in the community. Such religious values include caring for the more vulnerable in the community, i.e., the elderly, the sick, the children; mutuality wherein we evoke the African adage, "I am because we are and since we are therefore I am"; being each other's keeper in the sense of upholding one another in times of need, and mutual uplifting for more rejuvenation. The goal of reconstruction of such values is to promote and struggle for sustenance of life, protection of life, enhancement of life and enrichment of life (i.e., life in all its wholeness).

A communitarian ethic consistent with human dignity calls for deep remembering, a task requiring new schools of thought, new moral courage and new ways of learning from each other within, across and between our communities. It calls for new and creative ways and forms of sharing that deliberately transcend accustomed patterns of academic exchange and social interactions and seek to share life with life. It calls for new critical consciousness, as well as new interpretative skills and methods. Above all, it calls us to look at the 21st century with new eyes. It challenges us to form the new generation of African youth equipped to build our communities in which rights, justice and dignity will characterize the lives of our people in each and in all places. That is why it is the great task of the churches and other communitarian agencies to engage in the search for theological and moral paradigms for sustenance of life with dignity in sustainable communities.

The dominant themes of modernity, especially those linked to astonishing developments in technology, raise critical questions with regard to human dignity. The issue or issues at stake with respect to the apparent triumph of modern technology must be engaged contextually. There are certain existential dimensions of human experience that cannot be fully grasped or articulated through the use of technology. One may dare to contend that there are certain features of modern technology that reflect lingering aspects of the incompleteness and emptiness of human beings. Yet one cannot speak of a form of technology which displaces spirituality, even though there are forms that enhance the hedonistic tendencies of human nature. I would like to divide this subject into two basic categories: namely, the general ontological problem of science-based technology, and the historical context in which particular technologies are used and introduced as part of a larger political project.

Scientific inventions are by their very essence the means by which the phenomenon of existence is understood and replicated through technology. But the origin of ideas and their application is entirely based on imagination. The methods of science are a construct based on norms of precision by which empirically deducible, complex processes are simplified and put to practical use. Scientific inquiry is limited to the world of phenomena.

But the process by which abstract ideas are translated from the world of consciousness of being is unlimited by empirical concerns. Science achieves the highest level of authentication when it leaves open possible options outside the realm of empirical analysis. It is scientific to *restrict* the boundaries of science to the realm of dialectical empirical discourse. The method of the sciences must be flexible to include intuitive capacities of the mind and the power of imagination. After all, existence itself is not entirely a scientific construction, for within it there are ethical dimensions to relations among things that beg ontological responses. The context in which science operates is also subject to other constructs that do not necessarily have any affinity with the methods and norms of empirical investigation. For example, attempts to extrapolate the so-called dialectical method as normative for social and political processes have ignored any distinction between events that are proper objects of scientific inquiry and moments that are subject instead to the vagaries of human experience.

The dawn of modernity is often linked with certain ideological developments and the application of certain types of technology associated with scientific innovations, but in fact the reality of modernity is not mono-causal, nor is technology an exclusive feature of modernity. Technology is but one element in a more complex web of human endeavour. In the early 1960s, for example, enthusiasm for political self-determination had spread throughout the whole of Africa with a new fervour that defeated the European technologies of warfare and imperialism. This defeat of technologies came as a result of the centrality of the dignity around which human life is organized. In the struggle for liberation, Africa proved her ability to regain her political dignity in the face of increasingly intense applications of modern technology in the service of imperial interests.

As pointed out above, there is in the Western world a dilemma posed by the choice to be made between a human need for community and an environment that is hostile to the values of community. Where shall we find the kind of technology that not only affirms but enhances the dignity of human life? Can modern technology facilitate the theological and cultural renaissance which is vital for the survival of humankind in this day and age?

There are various theological and moral metaphors in the creative effort to reclaim human dignity. Liberation as a moral theme for Christian theological reflection has been explored through analysis of the Exodus narrative in the Old Testament. Moses emerges from this record as the leader who delivers the enslaved people of Israel from their bondage in Egypt. The narrative has been a source of inspiration and greatly appeals to people under oppression. For the African people, the liberation motif in the Bible has inspired struggles against slavery, colonialism and apartheid. Many a leader of the African liberation movements was seen as the "Moses" who motivates, mobilizes and leads the people from colonial bondage.

In the African diaspora, the fact that a century after the American civil war the African-Americans were still denied their civil rights led civil-rights activists in the 1950s and 1960s to elaborate a theological motif that would help them to mobilize the communities for change. Not only did the Exodus motif prove to be a powerful metaphor, it also provided a social framework for organizing. Leaders like Martin Luther King, Jr were popularly likened to Moses whose task it was to lead the people to the promised land. Theologians like James Cone and Gayraud Wilmore gave theological rationalization to the civil-rights movement.

However, both on the African continent and the diaspora alike, the historical moments that gave rise to the need for the liberation paradigm now have been replaced by other moments that require us to seek new paradigms. With the end of apartheid in South Africa, and the changing character of the socio-economic context in the USA, African and African-American theologians are challenged to discern theological paradigms for the 21st century. The prevailing socio-historical contexts require that we shift the paradigm from the post-Exodus to post-exile imagery, with reconstruction as the concomitant theological metaphor. This theme is being explored today by theologians like Jesse Mugambi.

Re-membering

Africa is and will remain for years to come the crucible in which are fused the ancient and the modern elements of human existence. The modern elements in the mix are those associated with the recent innovations of sophistication, from ideas to life-style, while the ancient elements are identified more with primordial values of human ancestry that are located among communities of memory. It is these communities, endowed with living memories of ancestral truths, that become the meeting place of primordiality and modernity. The labelling of communities in rural Africa as "tribal" and "pre-modern" tends to undermine their power as a living presence of the re-membering of a dismembered humanity.

The violence of imperialism, especially through slavery and colonialism, led to the dismembering of the Africans. We were scattered in the diaspora by the forces of domination and oppression. Just as it was in the Berlin conference in 1884-85 when Europe was united against Africa, so it is today that the unbridled global capitalist economy threatens the emergence and even the very survival of the communities of memory in Africa and those in the diaspora. Given the depth of the crisis, it is only through the resilience of the spirit, manifested in a sound and awakened consciousness, that Africans will live beyond the enduring limitations imposed by the Western-designed new global order.

History without memory leads to estrangement from the past and discontinuity with the future. Generations that are born today should be nourished with a deep and profound understanding of the heritage and traditions of sapience that constitute the moral fabric of our people. A generation needs to be endowed with critical consciousness to respond to incursions of other values communicated through the global information infrastructure. Education for critical conscious-ness is crucial in claiming a new vision for the future, based on the recovery of the past, in order to restore the present. The importance of re-membering what was dismembered cannot be over-emphasized. It is part of the process of bring-ing together that which has been scattered and lost. Part of the crisis of modernity is the growing trend of discontinuity and the death of memory.

Contemporary human beings irrespective of their social or global location are constituent parts of late modernity. Even if they claim to live outside the realm of modernity, they do so as a form of resistance to certain modern trends and values. But the descriptive value of the notion of moder-nity is, at best, a relative term applied to illustrate particular experiences of contemporary humanity. Such experiences may vary from society to society depending on historical progressions and conditions.

Modernity in Africa

The comparative advantage of Africa is that, while being assimilated by Western values and structures, resistance to European forms of modernity have been giving rise to new forms of African modernity. These forms of modernity are usually found outside state structures as a way of creating alternatives not only to European models of modernity but also as modes of surviving the tyranny of the state in Africa. Cultural resources drawn from primordial values become means of resistance, not just to affirm absolute autonomy but rather to negotiate relationships with the rest of the world.

This kind of resistance has been not just a series of nega-tions of European modernity but also ways to produce new forms of culture and value systems that have led to multiple identities on the continent. The fixation on tribal identity in modern post-colonial studies focused on Africa encourages a fallacy because the studies do not reflect the complexities underlying contemporary struggles and responses to European modernity. Communal values and ethnic identities are basic aspects of social reality that are an embodiment of African modernity. Yet no one can deny that tribal identity remains a universal form of basic, primordial identity which is in no way exclusive to Africa.

Attempts at mystifying primordial experience as exclusively African are part of the crisis of the Europeanization of cultures. The primordial condition is the basic human condition of being in the world, irrespective of culture, tribe or stage of development. That is why the problems of technology and the unburdening of cultural and moral obligations are universal phenomena. In the emerging social infrastructure, attempts at creating autonomous self-regulatory institutions of efficiency and excellence have been foiled by the problem of human fallibility. Corporate institutions which deny the human factor often get into trouble with their workforce. Automation cannot replace sound judgment, nor can the excellence of technology displace human compassion.

There are emerging on the continent today new forms of modern expressions of multiple identities that interweave historical memory with modern technology. Modern art forms and architecture reflect this blending. The migration of thousands of African professionals to the North, including scientists and entrepreneurs, is a great human contribution to the resources of growth and maturation in Western modernity. The fact that a good number of Africans are in senior positions in international institutions, and that there has been major growth in the intake of African students in prestigious universities all over the world – notwithstanding the question of brain-drain – cannot be ignored.

Agents of change

Let us now turn to the issue of human agencies for change and the challenges that undermine modernity. First we must understand the nature of globalization as a historical reality, and especially globalization in the African context.

The pulse of modern-day globalization is felt in the movement of capital from one part of the globe to another without checks and balances or mechanisms of accountability. Some Western scholars, such as Richard Longworth, describe this phenomenon as

> a revolution that enables any entrepreneur to raise money anywhere in the world and with that money to use technology, communications, management and labour locally anywhere the entrepreneur finds them, to make things he wants to sell anywhere there are customers.

Quoted by Richard Dickinson ed., *Economic Globalization,* see p.5

Such entrepreneurs are not accountable to local democratic structures or institutions, nor do they accept any ethical social responsibility, even in the event that their activities cause harm to the environment.

The other dimension of contemporary trends is the concentration of power in the hands of a few. There is a small circle of people in the whole chain of global media networks, and they influence the imaging of Africa to the rest of the world. Increasingly, corporate mergers extend their spheres of influence in nearly every aspect of our lives. Their inner logic is maximization of profit, regardless of any ethical considerations. This unbridled competitiveness leads to further concentration of power and exacerbates disparities between the haves and have-nots, rich and poor, within and between nations. The gap continues to increase and there is no means known within the system itself that could stop this madness!

Meanwhile, according to the United Nations Development Programme's (UNDP's) 1998 *Human Development Report*, the 15 richest people in the world enjoy combined assets that exceed the total annual gross product (GDP) of sub-Saharan Africa. At the end of the 1990s, the wealth of the three richest individuals on earth surpassed the combined GDP of the 48 least-developed countries.

As Fridah Muyale-Manenji writes:

> In Africa, women have mostly been involved in farming, in employment as civil servants, and in industry. They have also been involved in small-scale entrepreneurships. No doubt, these sectors have been severely affected by the introduction of trade liberalization. Women on this continent contribute the most critical factor in agricultural production and agriculture. Yet liberalization has failed to ensure the availability of credit, agricultural inputs such as fertilizers and insecticides at affordable prices. The marketing of their produce has been thrown in the hands of businessmen whose sole objective is profit maximization. The result – food security in Africa is highly threatened.
>
> "The Effects of Globalization on Culture in Africa in the Eyes of an African Woman"

Under the onslaught of globalization and structural adjustment programmes (SAPs) the average African family is unable to feed itself. A community that is reduced to begging for food is in danger of losing its most fundamental source of dignity. This is a new social phenomenon in Africa where even at the worst of times, save for natural disasters like protracted droughts or floods, people were able to feed themselves. Gone are the days when most African communities had a strong policy on food security evidenced by silos in each family compound. Today, most of these are empty – people have been forced into a situation where they are living from hand to mouth. Even the middle-class working elite have succumbed to the habit of using their wages even before they receive them.

Cultural globalization has seriously compromised the dignity and self-confidence of the African people at all stages of life. Muyale-Manenji is right in observing that the issue, amazingly, is that of ignorance. Even the rich and well-to-do have no clue about the system that has invaded the African continent. Or even if they are aware, they have either chosen to overlook the overall implications or have decided that they are also benefactors of the system... The youth prefer the Western beats to the local artists and hair-styles, shoes and clothing keep to the trends on the Western fashion scene.

This growing inequality is even more dramatic when we consider the pattern of consumption of the world's resources. The North with about one fifth of the world's population consumes 70 percent of the world's energy, 75 percent of its metals, 85 percent of its wood and 60 percent of its food (a good amount of which is wasted!). It is also further estimated that the North consumes the equivalent of the average consumption of 32 billion people whereas the world's total population today is barely six billion. The biggest paradox of today's global capitalist economy is that the creation of more wealth does not lead to alleviation of poverty. In addition, with poverty comes malnutrition, hunger and other vices derived from deprivation. It is estimated that nearly a third of the people in the least-developed countries – most of them in sub-Saharan Africa – will die before reaching the age of 40. In Africa, the average household consumes 20 percent less today than it did 25 years ago.

Resistance movements

Many conflicts arising in modern times are not isolated acts of anarchy but part of a frustrated grassroots response to the weakening and fragmentation of African society in the context of globalization. Let us consider the peculiar phenomenon of movements that use cultural and spiritual resources as a means of resistance against the tyranny of the state and the violence of globalization. The growth of these movements is exemplified by grassroots activists' resilience, demonstrating a cultural or spiritual immunity against the patronage and demands of the state (Alice Lakwena's Holy Spirit Movement is a classical example that endured a protracted struggle against dictatorships and the military states of Uganda). Most such movements cut across the gender prejudices of patriarchal societies and thus are not only counter-cultural but also revolutionary.

For example, the Mau Mau uprising which led the British to give up colonial rule in Kenya was initially a struggle to recapture land from the white settlers. Later, it became a symbol of national struggle against external domination. By fighting against the ownership and use of their land the people were seeking and reclaiming their existential freedom. When the colonial government was preparing to hand over the country at independence, a complicated million-acre settlement scheme was negotiated. This scheme was a product of two phases of development: the first colonial and the second neo-colonial. In the first phase, the colonial authorities tried to implement a settlement programme aimed at a very limited number of relatively prosperous Africans. It was designed, in fact, to favour not just any prosperous Africans, but specifically those who had been loyal to the colonial regime. In this phase, official thinking was guided by an unsophisticated view of both Kenya's society and its political dynamics. In the second phase, the authorities greatly expanded the scheme to offer benefits to Africans of certain classes and political tendencies. In skilfully dangling carrots and wielding sticks, the neo-colonial phase was marked by a more sophisticated understanding of Kenya's society and politics.

Another contemporary movement that has been likened to the nation of Islam in the United States is the Mungiki in Kenya. Mungiki is a coined Kikuyu word that denotes "the public" or "the plebs", the common people. It is probably derived from *muingi,* a term with a similar meaning. It has been an underground movement since 1985 and became a force in the political scene from December 1997 when sixty-three of its members were hauled into a local court and charged with administering an illegal oath, belonging to an illegal society and holding unlawful assembly. According to the founders, it was born when a number of people saw visions in which they were commanded by a divine power to call upon all Africans to go back to their roots and values. Mungiki advocate female circumcision, a practice that is outdated and against basic human rights. Interestingly, the group does not compel anyone to be circumcized. Mungiki argue that the mainstream church injunction against polygamy is un-African and so they are affiliated to mainstream Islam. They advocate polygamy as a remedy to prostitution and the problem of single motherhood and street children. They are vehemently against the use of contraceptives. The leaders of Mungiki claim that they have nothing against modern medicine and education. Modern education, it seems, is one of the positive attributes of "Western culture"; indeed, to survive in the modern world, one needs to identify with certain "cultural traits" of the Western world. The Mungiki claim they are non-political but at the same time insist on the right to call for change of bad government in order to attain justice and prosperity in society. They attribute glaring social disparities in Kenya today to systems which are modelled on Western values, "which promote individualism as opposed to the communal inclinations of Africans of days gone by".

In its teachings, Mungiki raises questions: What is the source of poverty? Why are there so many street children? They take issue with policies which do not promote employment. They believe that the worst thing ever to happen to the Africans was the coming of the European missionaries who taught of "their prophets and visions from foreign lands". They believe that Jesus Christ was a prophet for the Jews. "We Africans had our prophets like Mugo wa Kabiru, whose teachings we should have heeded." At Gitwamba, Mungiki keep a shrine enclosing a black memorial stone. The Mungiki do not believe in life after death or heaven or hell. They pray to Mwene Nyaga, always facing Mt Kenya, and hold prayers in the early morning and late afternoon. Members are taught not to smoke, so instead they take snuff. Alcoholic beverages are prohibited. At Githurai in urban Nairobi they are credited with having rid the neighbourhood of criminals who were terrorizing the residents at bus stops at night.

In a word, Mungiki is an exclusive and often confusing social movement, with neither a clear-cut programme of action nor a visible policy in terms of political change. It is a reactionary movement in terms of the tremendous political, social and economic changes that Kenya has undergone in the last two decades. Its message was conceived to appeal to members of the Central Province, where female circumcision was a rallying point against Christian missionaries in 1929, and where oaths were used to rally communities against real or imagined enemies. By virtue of its popularity among the electorate in populous Central Kenya, Mungiki is likely to be wooed by politicians in the run-up to the general elections in Kenya. The nature of their response will show whether Mungiki is indeed a movement for social change or an opportunistic social entrepreneurship led by unscrupulous individuals.

It is obvious that in addressing our subject matter, there is an urgent need for new instruments of social analysis that would equip scholars in Africa with more profound appreciation of the various forms of grassroots responses to post-modernism in Africa. People are becoming more confident as they begin to locate their experiences outside the constructions of Eurocentrism. The movement back to their own local situations is synergetic and may plant the seeds of new revolutions on the continent. This phenomenon may lead to a new way of doing politics in Africa as people recognize the irrelevance and unpopularity of the nation-state in its current form. The power of the state will then inevitably be balanced by the emerging authority of grassroots people's movements.

While the people are still being punished for refusing to obey state tyranny, the growth of alternative communities is increasingly becoming the utopian means of legitimate defiance. This could lead to creative innovations in a diversity of spaces. (One may compare what is happening among the movements of indigenous peoples, especially in Latin America; see esp. Esteva and Prakash).

A paradigm shift in the discourse of social change has become necessary by virtue of the gradual weakening of the nation-state. Familiar powers, long the centre of social gravity, are slowly but surely shifting to the periphery. It is more likely than ever before, especially in Africa, that disenfranchized and marginalized groups will acquire greater capacity for self-governance and ideological insulation from state tyranny as well as from divisive interventions of other forces that serve the interest of the agents of globalization. It is inevitable that a time is coming for new approaches to the articulation of grassroots initiatives that will genuinely rid African communities of their colonial mentality "hang-over".

The emerging post-cold war global order is taking shape within the context of ideological imports and universal trends of post-modernism. The meaning and use of power is transformed into a global phenomenon. Power is now used to exclude the weak from the resources associated with the excesses of global capitalist investments. This is best resisted by learning from the people themselves. It is in their stories and experiences, through images, metaphors, rituals, symbols, concepts and words, that what is emerging from the grassroots initiatives is both derived and preserved. This narrative provides a broader framework for the critical understanding that sometimes violence is the only means necessary for survival under state tyranny. It indicates how grassroots movements are sustained, sometimes by dodging the state, negotiating with it where appropriate, or by ignoring it entirely where it becomes irrelevant.

We are not unaware that occasionally these movements are obscured or even destroyed by aggressive assertions of tribal and sectarian identities. Nevertheless, one can speak of differentiated responses to post-modernism which, on the one hand, leads to the domination of the powerful via globalization, and to the tyranny of the state in Africa on the other hand. Grassroots communities are responding not only to the tyranny of the local state, which is immediate and visible, but also to the tyranny of the "global state" which is mediated and invisible. In the process, they show a high level of ecumenical maturity in their capacity to live with and celebrate difference.

Market economies driven by private enterprise and competitive democracy (the dominant economic and political features of neo-liberalism) are promoted in the language of post-modernism as constructs that now seek to control the whole world. Meanwhile, the politics of land distribution and violence, as shown in recent elections in Zimbabwe, are in every sense a classic example of how the state in its moment of tyranny still utilizes a legitimate plight of its people to manipulate affairs at the advent of globalization. Mere legal independence did not de-link the African nation-state from influences in policy and inherent interests of the former colonial powers. There is an uninterrupted continuum between the colonial and the global project. Thus, the relationship between democratization and violence takes different forms in different countries.

For example, as in the case of Rwanda, contemporary conflicts that have led to genocide are deeply rooted in the colonial past. That was the time when notions of tribe were created and, out of political expediency, linked to the acquisition and distribution of public resources. This is true for former settler colonies including Zimbabwe and other countries in southern Africa, especially with regard to the question of land. Colonization was but a stage in the development of imperialistic designs for global dominance. It is no longer cheap human labour nor open brutality of domination and grouping of tribes that is employed but the subtleties of an unjust international political and monetary regime applying the innocence of modern technology to craft a system of global governance.

While the corporate agents of globalization are not accountable to local democratic structures or institutions, a middle phenomenon in the civic public realm has emerged with new claims of legitimacy. The instruments of this phenomenon are mainly advocacy groups and NGOs (nongovernmental organizations) that are neither anchored in local communities nor accountable to the grassroots communities. Their claims should be closely examined vis-a-vis the social deficit exhibited by a weak, vulnerable and disenfranchized state.

In this regard, the survival of the nation-state in Africa may be better understood within the complexities and the context of the global project. Traditional studies and contemporary theological discourse on Africa often miss the critical link between various global processes and their grassroots responses to the prevailing political and economic crisis in Africa.

Globalization and Africa

Democracy is often perceived as an innocent instrument which, when used properly according to the rules of fairness and free play, would yield desired changes and ensure necessary checks and balances for political and social stability. At the dawn of globalization in Africa, the democratic project is signified more by turbulent electoral events than processes. The logic of the project is focused on episodes of competitive politics that give no guarantee for the preservation of human dignity and sustainable peace. Elections have become nothing but opportunities for the survival of a weak and disillusioned nation-state. They are a litmus test of the colonial features of the state and its capacity to appropriate elements of post-modernist constructs of social organization. The result too frequently has been endurance of old regimes with new faces of international legitimacy through hobbled elections.

In some instances, application of Western models of governance have led to violent destruction of state institutions and their replacement with other structures of self-governance, as in the case of Somalia. Somalia is a perfect example of defiance against the so-called international norms of civility and statecraft. It is to be remembered that it was Somalia that, while at war with herself, resisted violently the intrusion of Western powers on her soil. In spite of superior weapons and an elite military force, the United States of America succumbed to a shameful defeat by village militias.

The notion of ethnicity has been appropriated politically through violence in the struggle of the nation-state against the resistance of grassroots communities in some parts of Africa. Whenever the complexities of situations involving political transitions are not well managed, they bare the ugly face of the megalomaniac attitudes and tendencies of some leaders in Africa today. This may give rise to bigotry and disregard for Africans as backward and incapable of managing their own affairs. The idea of the oppressed oppressor does not do justice to the complexities underlying this kind of tyranny, which is begotten of another kind of sophisticated and less obvious form of oppression. In the absence of avenues to channel legitimate anger against the state and the agencies of globalization, a frustrated and disillusioned civil society may well engage in acts of social cannibalism, thus falling victim to self-inflicted violence. They will then blame themselves for the pain they experience, resulting in the twofold tragedy of external adversity and self-hatred.

The African leaders who took over from the British and French colonial regimes presided over the legal transition to majority rule, but most of them remained puppets of the royal crown and others mimicked the same strategies of divide-and-rule that were applied by their colonial masters as strategies of further self-entrenchment. Local institutions that then claimed autonomy from the colonial state were soon integrated into authoritarian structures of the day. Excluding others, leaders of prominent tribal communities were made part of government in order to silence popular dissent.

One would expect political violence in Africa to decline with the advent of the democratization process. Instead, politically motivated violence tends to be increasing and has become a recurrent characteristic in the run-up to general elections. Shocked at discovering their incredible unpopularity, long-serving heads of state in Africa sought to punish with impunity their peoples' refusal to be oppressed. Their reaction has come through state-instigated violence. During the cold war, most post-colonial leaders in Africa relied heavily on state institutions to fund political clientelism which was mainly supported by making alliances in the ideological war between East and West. These leaders played cat-and-mouse with the Americans and Soviets. All indications show that the situation now is likely to get worse before it gets better.

Even the coming of space explorations which seem to promote the innocent quest for other forms of life in the universe may soon be transformed to ensure exclusive access and control of resources in the cosmos for utility by the few centres of power in the globe. Just as the process of globalization began with the adventure of conquest within the terrestrial realm, so it is likely that space exploration will soon be guided by the same logic of commodification that once reduced other human beings to the status of items on sale and objects to be used for labour.

Technological advancement in space exploration, far from being inspired simply by the desire for knowledge, also has been motivated by expansionist policies of Northern nations. The "star wars" programme, for example, was initiated during the cold war.

Yet in the midst of such highly sophisticated scientific initiatives, people of the South are suffering under the yoke of diseases that threaten their very lives. Western medical research institutions, while patenting results from the South in the race to find a cure for AIDS, are not giving priority to the continent with their own discoveries, even on humanitarian grounds. Again the profit motive within global pharmaceutical industries with vested interests in ongoing research on AIDS takes precedence over ethical considerations! In this way, the predicament of human suffering becomes a means to establish a new industry serving the interests of the rich and powerful, shifting alliances whenever necessary as a way of consolidating power.

Some leaders like the late Mobutu Seseko of Zaire siphoned colossal amounts of money into secret accounts in Switzerland and used state resources for personal gain. They felt no accountability at all to the people they once claimed to serve. Such leaders maintained power with the help of Western and Eastern super-powers but without the authority of their people. Inevitably, this would change because of shifts in global power arrangements after the cold war. The external capital or political aid that was used to manipulate local situations for political gain was no longer available because the strategic interests of the West were now focused on the demilitarization of Eastern Europe and the unification of Central Europe.

A new world order

Power without property tends to become more tyrannical since access to public resources becomes more restricted as economies are weakened. State resources and public funds then become the source of sustenance, and military spending rises to enforce unjust rule. Political movements that are created to oppose the incumbent become frustrated and disintegrate under intimidation and the formation of new, competing parties within the opposition. To add to the confusion, one finds an opposition that is opposed to itself. Such is the murky environment in which grassroots communities can no longer find shelter from the state or the civil society when negative forces of globalization are unleashed.

A crisis such as that of Angola, in which external powers engaged Africans in senseless violence, shows that even when American or Russian interests have been compromised by history, Africans are still found licking the wounds of unending conflicts. Such conflicts have grown deeper by their very nature and extend beyond the self-interests of those who initiated them. They have become cancerous. The blurred and distorted vision of African leadership is certainly responsible for the apparent permanence of these conflicts. Apart from allowing themselves to be clients of foreign interests, some of these leaders have turned their nations into private institutions such that the only common face of the nation-state is symbolized by a flag, a national anthem and a strong military regime. Tribalization of politics and politicization of ethnicity have resulted in the creation of an environment in which many conflicts and even civil wars flourished.

The catalogue of atrocities in independent Africa is a very long one. A partial list includes the Biafran war in Nigeria, the bloodbath in Liberia, civil war in Somalia, Angola, Sudan, ethnic clashes in Kenya, the Eritrea/Ethiopian border conflicts, not to mention the genocide in Rwanda, the abominable atrocities in Sierra Leone and the most recent Burundi massacres. While, in some of the cases, retaining political power is a clear motivation for violence, in others it is the struggle for dominion over natural resources. The civil wars in Angola, Liberia, Sierra Leone and, more recently, the Democratic Republic of Congo have become self-financing through the sale of diamonds in the international market. That was the only way possible for the civil war in Angola to outlive the cold war. In the Liberian crisis, when the then head of state Samuel Doe promoted the pride of his tribe at the expense of national stability, he became a victim and was beheaded by one of his own faction. Paulo Freire articulates the dilemma and predicament of the ethnic colonial state in Africa more succinctly:

> As the oppressor minority subordinates and dominates the majority, it must divide it and keep it divided in order to remain in power. The minority cannot easily permit the luxury of the majority rule of the people, which would undoubtedly signify a great threat to their own hegemony.

Pedagogy of the Oppressed, p.38

With the end of the euphoria of independence, when the dust of victory had begun to settle, the leaders in Africa were faced with the formidable task of nation-building whilst using the borrowed tools of Western statecraft. The challenge before them was to create a cohesive society in which a national political and economic culture would re-emerge to serve the newfound sovereignty of the people. Their slogans were majority rule and home rule. But before they could craft a new vision for their young nations, they found themselves faced by the invincible forces of neo-colonialism.

These forces were ideologically fronted during the cold war and later consolidated into what is now aptly described as globalization. In other words, the post-independence leadership in Africa is a product of these realities and cannot be analyzed or understood outside the globalized historical framework that continuously informs their judgments and actions. Hence, any successful reconstruction of the state and of society must include a new approach to leadership formation and an alternative framework for doing politics based on an ethic of human dignity and using local resources.

Two issues were at stake during the struggle for independence in most African countries and they are still at stake today: identity and land. But the question of land ownership is too complex to be reduced to mere contention between tribal identities and their claims of territorial ownership. Mahmoud Mamdani has written:

> The claim that political ethnicity was a primordial identity has given way to an instrumentalist notion that it is manipulated by special interests. The claim that political ethnicity is an outcome of elite manipulation resembles the nationalist conviction that ethnicity (tribalism) was no more than a colonial prejudice.
>
> *When Victims Become Killers*, p.15

The challenge of political formation in Africa remains critical for any success in establishing responsible and accountable leadership. The first generation of leaders was formed through the processes of struggles for political liberation. Those leaders failed when it came to running the state in independent Africa, not least because neo-colonization proved too formidable a force for them to overcome. But it also became evident that effective and responsible governance required different skills and ability from those that had been required to lead a liberation movement.

The second generation of leadership in post-colonial Africa has been formed through the process of the so-called second liberation made possible by the end of the cold war. The period is also identified as a wave of democratization in Africa. A decade into multi-party governance reveals that the new leadership is as bankrupt as their predecessors when it comes to delivering justice, peace and economic prosperity to the majority of the African people. Like their forerunners, these new leaders exhibit the same traits of corrupt practices and ineptitude.

Current African leadership practices, coupled with the dominant neo-liberal thinking globally, seem to be leading to yet another false start in Africa. This calls for different political formation processes to provide for qualitative change in political leadership and governance in Africa. The ecumenical movement should feel challenged to contribute to the search for new and different means of leadership formation in Africa.

In my view, the leadership formation processes so far have been missing a vital ingredient – the ethical dimension. In the previous chapters, we emphasized the need for ethical undergirding in leadership and governance. Spiritual discernment could well be the unique contribution that the church could bring to the search for qualitatively different processes and sites of leadership formation. The WCC Special Focus on Africa provides a useful ecumenical framework and space for such a contribution to be offered. The third generation of African leadership will be qualitatively different only if its members are formed and informed within a new ethical framework.

7. Reconstruction and Renaissance

> In a fantastically rich country such as Namibia, which produces gold, diamonds, copper and uranium and has one of the richest fish beds in the world, babies are dying of malnutrition. In the age of globalization, the fish caught in Namibia are converted into pet food by the rich industrialized countries... babies are dying so that pets may have food.
>
> "Christianity, Poverty and Wealth in the 21st Century: Project of Heads of Agencies Network", Namibian Case Study Initiative

Reconstruction is not possible without translating the discourse on African renaissance into historical reality. We shall begin by tracing the tools and assets of this discourse and then introduce other dimensions of the ethics of life as the ecumenical input and response to a long-awaited renaissance. It is in this context that we need to promote a healthy dialogue on social transformation as the key to sustenance of life.

We shall therefore examine closely the elements of contemporary development paradigms, and explore alternative models that are nurtured by the principles of human dignity. The question of renaissance as part of the agenda for African reconstruction is timely. We shall trace its origin in the pan-African movement and consider its content and authenticity. There is also the question of new and promising leadership for the future of Africa, and the essential qualities of a new generation who are called to find courage for hope. The goal of reconstruction is the restoration of wholeness, and a recovery of the dignity and integrity of the African people. This is why we have pursued discourse on the meaning and value of human development.

For quite a long time, Africans from different walks of life have tried to discern new visions and imagine alternative ways of understanding and running the continent. We begin this chapter by revisiting the historical context in which such imagination of alternatives has progressively developed from the days of negritude to the dawn of the renaissance. As Adebayo Adedeji puts it, "While the old order was built on conflicts and their containment, the so-called new world order [is built] on competition and confusion; a new, benign and enlightened international order can only be rooted in the joint efforts of strong partners." How can Africa become a "strong" partner in this new disorderly world? How can Africa influence and provide leadership in the emerging international value systems and constellations? These are some of the questions that we shall grope with in imagining possible alternatives.

The African movements of intellectual resistance to the spirit and ideological propositions of colonialism were very much alive in the earlier part of the 20th century. These were not only engaged in the exercise of discerning the elements of colonial ideology and its vicissitudes but were also transformed into movements of restoration of confidence and identity among the African people. A good example of this was already mentioned: Anta Diop's work (see bibliography), which defines African identity in strictly sociological and materialist terms by giving a sense of being African in proper historical depth, rather than the metaphysical definition in Sedar Senghor's epistemological movement of negritude.

Negritude is "the warmth" of being, living, participating in a cultural, social and spiritual harmony. It also means assuming some basic political positions – that colonialism has depersonalized Africans and that therefore the end of colonialism should promote the self-fulfilment of Africans. Thus, negritude is simultaneously an existential thesis (I am what I have decided to be) and a political enterprise.

The onslaught of colonialism and its legacies of oppression in the African continent were so profound that its violence against culture has destroyed a people's self-identity. Excavating the origins of African civilization in ancient Egypt is not just to refute the argument that the black race has never produced any great world civilization but affirms that Europe itself owes immense cultural debt to Africa.

More than merely reacting against the unilateral and Eurocentric conceptions of the African contribution to world civilization as a late eventful predicament in history, Anta Diop provides a wider perspective of a universal history in which Africa is profoundly involved, transforming the backward cultures of antiquity in Asia Minor into early Hellenistic civilizations. At the heart of the movements of historical revision that sought to reclaim the dignity of the African people from the unwritten past was articulation of African confidence in the face of forces of alienation.

The African dream

Protracted struggles for independence were also nurtured by political philosophies that were in dialogue with progressive movements in the world. Kwame Nkrumah's *conscientism* and Nyerere's *ujamaa* were attempts at the development of an African state that was both a democratic and ethical institution facilitating the nourishment and flourishing of human life. This was ultimately the African dream. According to Nkrumah, this dream could be realized only in the political unity of the African people. For Nyerere, it was also to come with a culture of resilience and the economy of self-reliance. Both dreams were short-lived due to the intrigues of global politics and the unforeseeable dimensions of the cold war. However, the pan-African movement gave Africa the Organization of African Unity (OAU) and also a new political agenda and language of resistance.

As already mentioned, the OAU accomplished its mandate of leading African states to complete legal independence. Today, the people of Nyerere's Tanzania can be proud of Swahili, a language that unites them and enables them to sing through the storm of global capitalism even though their national economy is now at the mercy of the International Monetary Fund and the World Bank.

Ultimately, it is the ethical dimensions of the state as a public institution created through a process of participation and accountability to the people that will save Africa from the anarchy of the colonial state. Nkrumah's original utopian vision of a united Africa could never have been possible in the absence of a coherent framework within which Africans understand themselves. Neither is it possible, even as a dream, without collective self-determination rooted in African spirituality and existentialism.

Kwame Nkrumah prophesied a long time ago that no such thing as democracy would survive in isolation on the continent of Africa. Yet for his dream to survive, it must go beyond the far-fetched imagination of a federation of African states as a way of resolving the problem of ethnicity and statecraft; i.e., by grouping the Bantu, Nilotes, Nilo-hamites and the Cushites into separate nation-states. This would be like suggesting that after the Rwanda massacre the Hutus and the Tutsis should be separated into two distinct states.

The assumption here is that these conflicts are derived exclusively from perceptions of difference as immediate sources of animosity. The only way out of this simplistic notion of naked ethnicity as the source of conflict in Africa is to focus on the colonial coinage of such terms as tribes and their usage as ideological instruments to further the interests of an imperial and oppressive regime. There is nothing intrinsic to humanity about the notion of ethnicity, just as there is nothing intrinsic about the notion of race. Tribal identity is historical and not metaphysical. While everyone agreed that the settler prerogative had to go, not everyone was agreed that the "tribal" too was a colonial construct that needed to be done away with even after its bipolar twin "native" was disgraced. Anti-colonial nationalism was divided on this question. Radical nationalism as championed by Julius Nyerere, for example, was determined to reform citizenship consistently, both to de-racialize and de-ethnicize it (Mamdani, *Citizen and Subject*, p.14).

It is the legacy of the idea of tribe, not the consciousness of identity, that is in question here. Ethnicity must be deconstructed from being seen as a source of conflict so that it may become a resource of consent. The biggest challenge in this regard is how to make Africans and people of the world affirm diversity of identity as a gift of variety that is complementary rather than conflictual. This is an invitation to a broader ecumenical space in which diversity is celebrated.

The concept of celebration in the context of living with difference is deeply rooted in the tradition of consensus-building among most African communities; for example, the nomadic people of Gabbra. (Gabbra people live in northern Kenya and have close cousins in Ethiopia. They are known for their democratic way of running their community – see Aba Mollu, bibliography.) The fundamental question is, how do we appropriate the traditional value systems of self-governance into a discourse on modernity, contrasting Western dialectical modes of consensus-building in which difference is perceived as in conflict with status quo? The notion of ecumenical and participatory space is predicated upon the conviction that all are drawn into dialogue without the prerequisites of an autonomous centre. It is the life-generating values that are deeply rooted in the various traditions of ethical institutions in Africa that should become the point of departure in facing the issues of the time.

Life-giving values

The value of life itself transcends all doctrinal considerations, especially those that define or justify institutional differences! Conversely, it is the life-giving values professed by these institutions that eventually may lead to meaningful or reasonable consensus for the common good of society. How do we discern the possibility of a common ground of being in the absence of the possibility of visible unity within the artificial boundaries of the nation-state? Is it not the human condition, the condition of depravity, of marginalization, of exclusion that creatively draws these institutions of people (also called tribes) to the table of dialogue, pleading "come, let us reason together"?

There is great value in reconstructing the African traditional philosophy that defines the individual as meaningful only in relation to the others. Outside of such interwoven relations, the individual person, however materially rich, is actually a nobody. To be is to be in good relationships with the others in the community. Such an understanding of the quality of being ought to be built into the vision of democracy for Africa. Such a vision must embrace the commonality of spiritual heritage and the cosmology of African people whose heart is defined by the kindred spirit and the inalienable value of life.

Africans are a people grounded in the force of life. The universe presents itself not only as an object of rational inquiry but also as a labyrinth of the ineffable presence of life everywhere. The crisis of meaning and confidence that is experienced by people in wealthy nations of the West is not common among young people in rural Africa. Lack of basic comforts is the dominant experience among the rural poor, but there are also the non-market values of abundant life apparent in a moral universe, even in the midst of poverty. The relational value of all life in the cosmos, especially the network of human relations, is sustained by a profound affection for the integrity of life.

It is this deep realization that human existence is incomplete without relationships that ultimately constitutes the flourishing of life for most Africans. It is not in the madness of commodification and appropriation of material goods at the expense of human relationships and relationship to all life in the cosmos. So the state, which ought to be guided by the values within society, must guarantee at least fair, if not equal, access to the life-giving and sustaining resources that are not subject to market mechanisms or regulations.

This quest for equality is deeply rooted in human dignity. It calls for great sacrifices and selflessness. The ethic of life is connected by grace with that which connects people to their ancestry, existence and pre-eminence. Land, trees, birds, air, sea, fish, sunshine, stars, moon, human beings and even insects are part of the generosity that life bequeaths upon us all. All these subsist on the ground of being, as signified by the land from which no human being should be alienated. Human and peoples' rights are therefore to be based on an ethic of accountability rather than impunity, inclusiveness rather than exclusion, participation rather than manipulation, dialogue and consensus-building (learned from African traditional values) rather than domination, solidarity rather than survival of the fittest, sufficiency rather than greed, equality rather than exploitation, liberty rather than captivity, and caring for life rather than destruction of life.

Unless and until the human dignity of every individual person is affirmed, respected and upheld, the democracy we are trying to build in Africa will be hopelessly truncated. In a capitalist economy, to be is to have money; indeed, you become an even higher being because you consume. From the African traditional point of view, the individuality of a person, as created by God, is all that matters to be valued for one's relations with others. One's dignity and worth do not, therefore, depend upon one's monetary wealth.

For a decade now, African politicians and the elite have been too much preoccupied with democracy as a form and as a process. To establish genuine democracy in Africa it is necessary to take a hard look at, and deal very intentionally with, the content and the relational character of democracy; that is, democracy as a way of life. Until and unless the African elite is liberated from the captivity of using the democratization process as a stepping stone to political positions of power, democracy is in danger of being stripped of its value.

That would be a repeat of what happened during the attainment of political independence in the 1960s. Instead of trying to discern the possibilities and potentialities in the new historical situation for societal alternatives, the political leaders saw the situation as one of opportunities to be seized to fulfill their own egoistic interests. In the rush to grab the spoils of the cold war, even the intellectuals abandoned their role of helping to articulate the rich experiences acquired during the many years of struggles against the social injustices in the society. Instead they opted for appointed positions in the unjust system, or rushed to occupy spaces created in the emerging opposition political parties and the proliferating non-governmental organizations.

African values in the quest for democracy

What added value is brought by the African traditional concepts and practices to the quest for modern democracy? There are at least four main elements: integrity and wholeness such as the whole person, the whole community, whole relations and the whole life. We need to move from an alienated state to a state of wholeness and reconciliation, to move from alienation in regard to one's culture and community to wholeness. Secondly, the relational dimension of democracy denotes being in, and belonging to, the community. There is a reciprocity of rights and responsibilities between the individual and the community. The third element of "added value" is consensus-building as a way of reaching decisions. The fourth element is equality in which hierarchical ordering of the society is subordinated to the higher notion of a horizontal dimension in people's relations. As we have already pointed out, the institution of the chief as one "above" the people was an imposition of colonial rule in Africa. Subsidiarity, which was common in most of the African communities, made it impossible for leaders to lord it over the rest of the people.

To bring about meaningful democratic change in Africa, it will be critical to introduce a moral dimension hitherto completely overlooked. The democracy we seek must be concerned not just with electoral matters, but also with the economic conditions of the majority of the people. It has to be a democracy that considers the unnecessary suffering of the people as being morally wrong and therefore unacceptable. The church in Africa has a major social responsibility in the democratization process that would lead to equitable distribution of resources in Africa. The church should seek to promote democracy as a vision, basic elements of which are freedom, equality, justice and fullness of life.

The relational dimensions must be a major ingredient of this vision. For Africa, the community is a social tapestry of relationships which sustain the life of each and all the members of the community. But the question then remains, what is the framework for the recovery and reconstruction of African heritages of integrated governance? Such a framework, based in dignity and integrity, cannot ignore the communitarian ethic of human existence essential to African societal and ethical value systems.

The triumph over apartheid and the subsequent democratic election of Nelson Mandela as president of South Africa is seen today as a defining moment in the renewal of a new vision for Africa. Mandela's successor, Thabo Mbeki, in his *Africa – the Time Has Come*, sees the new epoch as one ushering in the historical opportunity for African renaissance.

However, this revival of the African dream in South Africa is blurred by the hobbled nature of the democratic experiments elsewhere in the continent which do not seem to appropriate the culture, identity and reality of the African people. This makes it difficult to translate their plight into a meaningful discourse of resistance to global corporate capitalism. The alternative for Africa has always been to remain on the brink of uncritical adaptation of the continent to the emerging forms of global political and economic dispensations, which of course are devoid of authentic expressions of resilience and the soul of her people. In this context, we shall now examine the contemporary imaginations of alternative possibilities contained in the African renaissance project.

Since he took over the mantle of leadership from Mandela in South Africa, Mbeki has rightly been described as a disciplined manager whose understanding of modern trends in global politics and economics is highly commendable. Mbeki was the key political force behind Mandela's government adopting the free-market paradigm of growth, employment and redistribution of national resources. He played a pivotal role in the discernment and application of the reconstruction and development programme in South Africa as part of the broader context of renaissance. It is in the context of global trends and the deep concern for the reconstruction of the continent that the concept of renaissance is to be understood.

African renaissance

What is African renaissance, and to what extent can it translate into the reality of normative experience among the African people? The strategies by international financial institutions (IFIs) to do away with the state-led development paradigms, and overcome the problems of stagnation through the so-called open and free-market competition with minimal state intervention, has led to economic disasters in sub-Saharan countries. Today there is widespread poverty and disintegration of the social safety-net structures and the moral fabric of social equanimity, which is the foundation of community life in Africa. In fact, under the prevailing economic regimes proposed by the IFIs, the real GDP in Africa fell by 42.5 percent between 1980 and 1990 (UNDP, 1999 report).

The contemporary situation indicates a new phase of global corporate capitalist expansionism and control of large markets through the revolution in communication technology. The virtual take-over of the economic policies and programmes of the less powerful and poor countries by the IFIs is what characterizes the gradual weakening of the nation-state and the loss of state sovereignty in Africa. This situation is further aggravated by the fact that all African countries are deeply integrated into the world trade system in which it is impossible to compete or even get concessions for fair quotas under the contemporary trade regimes of the World Trade Organization. The continent is, to a very large extent, going through a process of economic enslavement. It is in this context that the prevailing imagination of the alternative, namely African, renaissance is taking place.

The idea of renaissance has a historical dimension and, as Mamdani has rightly observed, is a child of pan-Africanism – whose movement, as earlier demonstrated, sought to regain African dignity and humanity as a response to slavery and colonialism. Nkrumah's dream of the 1960s and even Mobutu's *recours à l'authenticité* (recourse to authenticity) are some of the later manifestations of the search for the authentic African identity. Nkrumah's vision could be described as the initial yearning for a political renaissance, which would include the consolidation of all the synergies towards unity of the African people. This did not preclude the search for authenticity nor did it overlook the urgency for economic well-being on the continent. The renaissance of

Nkrumah's time was defined by the primacy of the political question – the quest for a united self-determination of Africa.

It was Mbeki's speech in the South African parliament in May 1996 entitled "I am an African" that invoked a great deal of attention to the apparent crisis of authenticity, i.e., is South Africa part of Africa or of Europe? Inadvertently, Mbeki was also addressing a key theme as to whether the new leadership in democratic South Africa would become distanced from its popular roots and pushed into a globalizing perspective which marginalizes its own immiserated classes and immiserated continent.

Mbeki's speech could be described as an Africanist interpretation, which sought to employ a new language to construct an alternative history, identity and cultural dispensation of the South African people. Yet in this attempt, Mbeki is caught in the hermeneutic problem of situating what is uniquely African in the context of globalization, as if the existence of the former is completely hostage to the moment of the latter.

The debate on renaissance draws certain elements from Senghor's concept of negritude, Kwame Nkrumah's *conscientism,* Mobutu's *recours à l'authenticité* and Nyerere's call in 1967 for *ujamaa na kujitegemea.* It can therefore rightly be claimed that the concept of African renaissance has had many faces in the historic journey of hope towards a more dignifying future for Africa.

According to Ian Taylor and Paul Williams, since 1996 when Mbeki started to play a more active role in the formulation of Pretoria's foreign policy South Africa's African policy has coalesced around the notion of African renaissance – although Mbeki did not publicly use the term until an address to an American audience in April 1997. He had also addressed this topic in an earlier document entitled "The African Renaissance: A Workable Dream" which was released by the office of South Africa's deputy president. It suggested five areas of engagement with the African continent, namely, the encouragement of cultural exchange; the emancipation of the African woman from patriarchy; the mobilization of youth; the broadening, deepening, sustenance of democracy; and radical initiation of sustainable economic development.

Since then, Mbeki has sought to place South Africa at the forefront of solving Africa's problems through his advocacy of the renaissance concept. At its core, the notion of renaissance appears to be about maximizing South Africa's strategic optimism on the continent.

In an address at the UN University in April 1998, Mbeki expanded on some of the core elements that formed the substance of his renaissance vision which could be summarized thus: there are needs to establish and maintain systems of good governance, to introduce new economic policies which seek to create conditions that are attractive to the private sector, to reduce state ownership of the economy and to build modern economies. In addition, he argues for establishment of regional economic arrangements to lessen the disadvantages created by small markets and to introduce policies that would ensure access to good education, adequate heath care, decent housing, clean water and modern sanitation. At this stage, in spite of the impassioned rhetoric, the essential features of the renaissance and how to encourage its development remain vague.

In this rendition, the African renaissance points to Africa as an expanding and prosperous market alongside Asia, Europe and North America, in which South African capital is destined to play a special role through the development of trade and building of strategic partnerships. But the notion of economic expansion from the South has been perceived as rather triumphalist, with most East, West and Central African countries unwilling to embrace fully the renaissance project. In exchange for acting as the agent of globalization, South Africa appears to profit from preferential positioning in disposing of its largesse in minerals and mining.

It seems that the ideology that lies at the heart of Mbeki's notion of renaissance has become so deeply embedded within the globalized power structure that its proponents can claim with credibility that the values it represents have become self-evident – it is a political appeal to the yearnings of the South African middle class and civil society, placing South Africa in the forefront of emerging ideological dispensations for Africa. Mbeki's definition of renaissance neatly reflects the perceived need by weaker governments' elites to turn their countries into competitive states designed to attract the panacea of foreign investment.

It is openly admitted that this version of African renaissance accedes indirectly to the neo-liberal agenda of what constitutes post-modern economic policy for the continent, i.e., private-sector-driven reforms targeting foreign investments and a modern infrastructure to support a middle-class economy. President Mbeki and the protagonists of African renaissance have been pushing for a global initiative to provide debt relief for Africa and the introduction of new measures to encourage a larger flow of capital into the continent through foreign investment. This involves lobbying for reasonable trade policies to create international market access for African products and an assurance that Africa can eventually occupy her due place in the family of nations.

Mbeki's definition of the African renaissance is thus, to a very large extent, a projection of the liberalization of markets, deregulation and regional trade. His prescriptions clearly reflect the orthodox view in both contemporary development discourse and international economics. Indeed, it has been observed that they seem to reflect the arguments made by the World Bank and other donors who would like to see South Africa take a leading role to facilitate collective economic liberalization across the region by improving conditions for a more active role by agents of the private sector. As a result, many feel ambivalent towards the ideological content of Mbeki's renaissance.

Authentic renaissance

African renaissance as an ideological instrument in the restoration of dignity and democracy in Africa must therefore be rescued from the agents of globalization. It must be broadened beyond the South African agenda for Africa and evolve into a movement, galvanizing the whole sphere of African identity and modernity. The discourse on African renaissance must not only be based on memories and possibilities but on the ethic of human dignity derived from African traditional values and cultures that gave assurances and guarantees and minimized the anxieties of individuals regardless of their station in society. It is the heritage that is grounded on the value of integrity and dignity of every individual person in that no one need go hungry when the rest of the community has food. Authentic renaissance must lay down the foundation for democracy as a way of life, so that the whole body of social systems and constructs are subject to ethical evaluation. African renaissance also must be contexualized within the larger framework of historiography and global mapping of the continent. Only then will "renaissance" become a process of reclaiming and proclaiming abundant life for all in the community of human beings in Africa.

The late Mwalimu Julius Nyerere once said that peace was another word for development. Development is about peace, it is about abundant life, it is about justice and it is about happiness. In a word, development is about wholeness of life in sustainable communities.

As already emphasized above, wholeness is an essential notion in African community life. Whole person, whole community, whole life are critical to the understanding of abundant life. Over the years the concept of life's wholeness has been lost. Reconstruction of wholeness is therefore considered as essential in discerning a theology of development in Africa today. God as the source of peace is to be at the centre of development. Without God, there is no peace because God is understood to be the condition for peace. For the church, Jesus is the prince of peace. Combined with justice and righteousness, therefore, peace became possible through the covenant with God to lead a moral life. This concept takes the idea of God's preferential option for the poor a step further – God is seen as the ground of peace and justice and by extension the ground of human development. Authentic development cannot occur outside the common ground of being. We cannot continue our discourse on development without a serious critique of its theological and ecumenical implications.

A theology of development

By equating peace with development and accepting that God is the ground of peace and justice, and therefore also of genuine human development, an African theology of development introduces a cosmological dimension. The concept becomes more holistic and value-based. We infer from this that professionalism and technical aspects of development are not considered as critical as the ethos of development. This approach is critically concerned with essentials of both material and moral life. Knowledge and skills acquired by individuals are therefore considered as part of the community goods and not restricted to the inner being of the professionals. It is this understanding of mutual communal responsibility that makes it difficult for an ordinary African person in a rural community to understand why we must spend so much money paying consultants to do what those in the community are obliged to do – provide service to the people as part of structuring mutuality.

A brief revisit of the ecumenical debate on development of the 1970s and 1980s is vital. In particular, we shall take a close look at the impact the church had in the shift of paradigms and then identify issues being raised by young African theologians. This is significant in that the previous theological discourses on development did not seriously take into account the voices of young African theologians and women. The African women theologians bring in a new dimension which is a further invitation to critical discourse, namely, to cultural hermeneutics. For their part, the young African theologians' input provides a strong critique of the negative impact of globalization.

Genuine development occurs when people in their contexts begin to articulate and implement their own initiatives for cultural and communal regeneration or transformation.

Experience of the last four UN development decades has shown that global thinking and global solutions do not work at the grassroots level. What those decades have succeeded in doing is to enrich a small minority of people within and between nations. Concomitantly, they have also succeeded in condemning the majority of the people, especially in the South, to deeper levels of poverty and despair.

The UN development decades put economic programmes above everything else. Economic globalization has gone even further and made finance and trade sacrosanct. Human beings and the value of life are subordinated to finance and not vice versa. It is imperative that in the third millennium we emphasize the paradigm of development as liberation and social reconstruction and consider our mission as that of enabling the people to gain the capacity to refuse to be seduced by global capitalism and to be controlled by economic laws. The ecumenical movement is called to facilitate people in rediscovering and reinventing their local community so that the economy is integral to society and culture. The ethical dimension of development must be built into new development paradigms. By "ethical" we do not mean simply what is wrong and what is right; we refer to the collective memory of what has impacted the lives of people positively as well as negatively and how that memory enriches and informs our actions today as well as better preparing us to act differently in future.

In 1968 at its Uppsala assembly, the World Council of Churches committed the ecumenical movement to deepen and strengthen its solidarity with peoples of under-developed countries. The primary programme through which the WCC would be deeply involved in development work was to be the Commission on the Churches' Participation in Development (CCPD). From the early 1970s, the CCPD carried out a highly spirited programme through which the meaning, purpose and form of processes of development provided the foci for churches' development agenda.

Here I would like to identify the main features that provided a shift in the concept of development. The failure of the first UN development decade (1960-70) becomes obvious when development is measured against the lived experiences of poor people in concrete situations. The socio-economic conditions for the majority were many times worse at the end of the first development decade then at its start. The deeper the people of the South got involved in the development debate, the more it led to critical questions about the very concept of development. It is this reality that challenged the ecumenical movement to look more critically at the concept of development as understood in the discourses within liberal economics as well as in the UN system.

Ecumenical reflections increasingly led to the conviction that, in the name of development, many national and international economic structures were perpetuating or even reinforcing structures of injustice. Given the enormous strain on the environment, which growth models of development implied, and in the face of increasingly visible signs of the earth's limited resources and capacities, many began to question whether the ideals of development were suitable goals.

The concept shift was reflected in three new emphases: liberation, participation, and peoples as the subject of development. Liberation was seen especially by ecumenical ethicists as a more holistic and biblical concept than development. Consequently, if seeking liberation were substituted for development, then social and political issues would also be addressed alongside economic ones. Carried to its logical conclusion, liberation denotes social justice which is now generally accepted as a critical factor in any genuine human development.

The participation of the people

By the mid-1970s, participation became part of the ecumenical vocabulary. It was through participation that people could be seen to be subjects in earnest. At the centre of this premise is the argument that justice should be not merely distributive but participatory as well. This notion counters the one in liberal economics which encouraged concentration of power rather than its distribution.

The linkage between development and democracy in this notion is apparent. At the WCC's Nairobi assembly in 1975 and in subsequent years, the linkage was made more explicit in the theme of "Development: A Struggle towards a Just, Participatory and Sustainable Society (JPSS)". Though JPSS remained basically a concept and was not translated into a programmatic thrust in the following twelve years or so, its basic elements are reflected in the ongoing WCC programme on justice, peace and the integrity of creation.

The "people dimension" in ecumenical thinking was greatly influenced by the ideas and work of Urban Rural Mission (URM). The URM focused sharply on people as having countervailing powers so that the role of the ecumenical movement was to help them realize that potential. What the new ecumenical concept of development emphasized was not participation in general, but priority was put on participation of the oppressed and marginalized people who hitherto had been written off and pushed to the periphery as mere pawns in the development arena. It sought to place greater significance on what was seen as peripheral, rather than what was at the "centre". Added to the ecumenical vocabulary during that period was "God's preferential option for the poor" which provided the biblical basis for emphasis on marginalized and excluded people.

To articulate the concept shift even more clearly, the ecumenical movement adopted a new definition of development, quoted in *Betting on the Weak*: "The development process should be understood as a liberating process aimed at justice, self-reliance and economic growth. It is essentially a people's struggle in which the poor and the oppressed are and should be the active agents and immediate beneficiaries". This definition was a reversal of processes of accelerated modernization termed "development" in the post-colonial period. The process was determined by economic, political and technocratic links between the elite in the South and their partners in the rich countries. There was need to propose a development process that was mainly inspired and carried by the people themselves.

Already in the mid-1980s, the ecumenical movement was questioning the concentration of wealth in the rich countries and was critical about the structures that enhance further concentration. The interesting point to note is that IMF policies were blamed for having led to "international food disorder and hunger-related diseases" in developing countries (*The International Finance System*). The policies of this institution have continued to bring misery in developing countries, as during the Asia crisis of 1997. The churches and the ecumenical movement were urged to go beyond pointing out the unethical consequences of the decisions made by global institutions to concrete actions.

Today the problem of increasing world inequality, poverty, unemployment and environmental destruction has not been resolved. This situation has created worldwide protest by the civil society. The project of globalization has brought more negatives than positives, as statistics and life experience show.

The World Council of Churches raised this issue during its eighth assembly in Harare, Zimbabwe, in 1998: "The logic of globalization needs to be challenged by an alternative way of life of community in diversity." Churches were called to reflect on this issue. How much have we done today to resolve the issue of ownership both between nations and between people? Why should the top three billionaires in the world hold assets worth more than the combined GNP of all 48 least-developed countries (LDCs) with their population of some 600 million? Why should 19,000 people in the poor countries die daily of poverty-related causes? Why should the world have three billion poor people in the midst of so much wealth? ("Poor" in this last respect means one who survives on US$1 per day.) Why should the gap between the rich and the poor continue to widen? Why is there no political will to change things, and how long do we want to see people dying and destruction of the environment continuing?

These questions must be at the centre of our mission and must be asked and answered by churches and the ecumenical family as we continue our journey together during the early years of the third millennium. The need to adopt a truly integrated approach to development cannot be over-emphasized. Development in its current usage does not adequately capture and define what is implied by "integral approach". Formerly, the idea of development has been too anthropocentric. Now we must look at development in more cosmological and holistic terms.

An integrated approach

There are two fundamentals in an integrated approach to development. In spite of the astronomical advances human beings have made in science and technology, a corresponding advance in the art of just human relations remains a distant dream. The communication revolution has reduced the world to a small village where knowledge about one another is but a digit away. Yet human beings do not know how to live with one another even within the same community. The sense of insecurity has invaded the lives of human beings right in their communities and even families. The source of the insecurity emanates from none other than fellow human beings. Death from starvation in the midst of plenty is a reality not only in poor countries but even in industrialized countries, including the USA, the richest country on earth. Today third-world characteristics such as street sleeping and begging are common in the metropolitan areas of Europe and North America. A new ecumenical vision must seek to "strengthen processes which heal broken relationships and enhance the viability of human communities". Only then may we claim to have begun the meaningful reconstruction of the concept of development.

The wholeness and fullness of human life and that of the rest of the creation is a vision which also promises the inclusiveness of all; in turn, this challenges the process of globalization which tends to promote exclusion and fragmentation. It is a vision embracing the African concept in which the worthiness of individual persons is measured not by their capacity to consume but by the quality of the relationships between them and their fellow human beings. That is what makes each one say with confidence, "I am, because we are, and since we are, therefore I am."

This also means that the fullness of life promises safety not for a small minority but for all, just as the whole flock finds enough pasture in God's grazing field. In such a context where genuine caring for life and for one another is a matter of course, knowing each other becomes truly possible. The knowledge is, in this case, more than just casual acquaintance; it means to understand each other, making it possible to feel the weight of one another's problems and needs. When one's knowledge of the other's problem reaches that level, sharing becomes more meaningful and the wholeness of life is restored for all. This wholeness of life is not limited to the lives of humans only but is for all creation. Development in the third millennium must be all-embracing and all-encompassing.

The second key element for development in the 21st century is the need to be fully aware of economic and cultural colonization. We must be deeply concerned about the ideological dimension of contemporary globalization. Globalization carries with it assumptions and values that need to be questioned.

Globalization homogenizes as it hegemonizes. In the globalization discourse, a lot has been said about the homogenization of production and consumption. However, the discourse and analyses of globalization have said a great deal less about another consequence of globalization: hegemonization or the emergence of a hegemonic centre.

Thirdly, there is renewed need to affirm anew the critical importance of rooting ecumenical commitments in biblical and theological soil. The consequences of homogenization and hegemonization of economic globalization were not lost on the 4000 participants at the WCC's assembly in Harare. Alarming accounts of individuals and groups participating in workshops there delivered a clear message – the World Council of Churches needed to take action against the devastating social and ecological effects of economic globalization.

Fourthly, it is necessary to carry out a critical analysis of developmentalists' debt to the poor. The poor entered the development arena with a hoe and came out of it with a hoe, only this time it had a broken handle. Modernity, the ecumenical movement included, owes an apology to the poor for wasting their hope. In all parts of the world, the poor and marginalized peoples put their trust in international organizations and experts who promised to deliver them from their poverty and misery through the magic formula of development.

The ecumenical movement too fell under the spell of this magic. To that extent, we too have let the people down. Their hopes and aspirations were even higher when the promise for better life came from people of faith. The hegemonic designs of the cold war so dominated the affairs of the people of the world that even the best-intentioned initiatives were hijacked and re-directed to serve the interests of the super-powers. Reconstruction of trust and confidence in this respect now becomes a prerequisite for a new social contract between international organizations and the people at the grassroots in Africa.

Designer development led not only to disempowerment but also to dismemberment. Many ordinary people in the villages and towns are still going through the pain of dismemberment of their communal conviviality and traditional ideals of hospitality. Traditional knowledge and practices are not acquired easily. They take generations to form and in most cases are a result of empirical living: real experience, by real people, in real situations.

The challenge of facilitating solidarity and structuring mutuality in partnership between the people of Africa and funding agencies is critical to reconstruction. Very often we talk of solidarity being extended by the donor to the donee – solidarity here expressed vertically from the North to the South. We must go beyond this concept of solidarity and talk of mutuality because vertical forms of partnership lead to one-sided vulnerability. One of the essential characteristics of partnership is mutual vulnerability, whether we are talking in social terms (marriage, deep friendship, etc.) or in economic terms (business enterprises). Even the story-telling that has been embraced as a sound methodology leads to the vulnerability of the storyteller (South) but normally is not reciprocated on the part of the listener (North). But if the partnership is horizontal as well, then there is likelihood of greater resonance between stories of the peoples of the South and the social realities of the people of the North. Mutuality becomes real and meaningful. Partnership and vulnerability are shared.

Social transformation as seen by women and young theologians

New ways of doing theology must constitute an essential element in social reconstruction of Africa. The ecumenical movement is both challenged and called to accompany women and young African theologians who are today capable of bringing a fresh approach to the discourse of transformation. Voices from the Circle of Concerned African Women Theologians (the Circle) and Young African Theologians are deeply enriching discourses on theology of development and mission in the 21st century. The Circle is calling for both biblical and cultural hermeneutics as the condition for any process of healing, well-being, empowerment, justice and liberation for women. In that view, one should not separate development issues from theological empowerment processes.

That also means it is essential to articulate how religion and culture play significant roles in the way women understand their place in society, including development. In other words, they expect a theologically educated person to be equipped to see how all aspects of life – politics, economics, religion, social and cultural – affect the individual and the community. However, such analysis is not complete without gender analysis. According to Nyambura Njoroge:

> Any cultural and religious activity that hinders the well-being and dignity of women, no matter how well entrenched in the life of the community (for example female genital mutilation, wife

inheritance, polygamy), is condemned. This is not to say that all women agree on this but those who do not accept such practices have written very strongly against them.

Njoroge argues that since 1989 when the Circle of Concerned African Women Theologians was launched in Accra, Ghana, African women theologians have clearly and loudly expressed their concerns on patriarchy and sexism and culture.

Another aspect that is crucial for women is the issue of power. Increasingly, many women are acknowledging their powerlessness even when they hold positions that may appear powerful, because it still requires a lot of effort to be heard and taken seriously, not to mention the hard work which went into obtaining that position in the first place. Unfortunately, the experience in ecumenical institutions is hardly any different from other organizations. The Circle members are concerned that patriarchal leadership styles (even when practised by women) are almost always hierarchical and very disempowering to women in particular and the marginalized in general.

In light of this, the second pan-African conference of the Circle in 1996 focused on the theme "Transforming Power". According to Musimbi Kanyoro, this has a double meaning – power that transforms and power that needs transforming because it is abusive and destructive. At the centre of this discussion is violence against women and girl children, a topic which has received minimum attention by many churches in Africa. Violence is a big hindrance to the development of women, girls and communities, and it will be a concern for the Circle for many years. The wider ecumenical movement is challenged to accompany the Circle in this journey.

For a biblical understanding of social transformation to be relevant and contextual it must be informed by a critical socio-historical analysis. Young African theologians consider globalization to have an adverse effect on genuine human development. Economic globalization concentrates power in fewer hands, making it more difficult to realize distributive justice both within and between nation-states. To the extent that economic globalization leads to fragmentation at the community level, even the little gains made in churches' participation in development are under threat. Our understanding of the effects of globalization will therefore impact the way we articulate our theology of development in the early decades of the 21st century.

The young African theologians are critical of globalization as a neo-liberal market model that generates benefits for the few while condemning the rest of humanity to being objects in a system that impoverishes and disempowers them (for example, the consultation on "African Theology in the Context of Globalization", Ghana, 2002). Globalization undermines the role of the nation-state and further weakens the family as an entity in the African community. The skewed distribution of power in the hands of the few and unfair trade policies that demand liberalization of Africa's economies, while the North practises protectionism, is a hallmark of this process.

The crux of the problem of the process of globalization lies in its inherent socio-economic injustices that have resulted in and continue to impoverish the poor. Globalization, like slavery, is an oppressive system that denies people their right of economic and social independence, indeed their right to life and development. Its commodification of life and its unethical measurement of life only in dehumanized economic parameters of profit cannot go unchallenged. Theology might not provide all the answers in the fight against globalization, but it can provide the social framework within which to offer alternative ethical responses to the process.

In analyzing the socio-political implications of globalization in Africa, the young African theologians at the Ghana consultation were convinced that the key to the mechanism of globalization is its tendency to create anarchy within society. The sad paradox of Africa as a deeply religious continent and yet the one afflicted by some of the world's worst politically motivated violence was one issue under discussion.

The consultation attributed the social instability, the spread of HIV/AIDS and a multiplicity of social ills mainly to the negation of *ubuntu*: the slide from the traditional respect for the sanctity of life and the advent of a new global culture that sees people as objects rather than subjects. The worldwide spread of information technologies and Western values was seen as signalling the annihilation of local heritage and habits. Theology, it was contended, has to start from the traditional family, then rise to national levels, then to the global community, rather than taking globalization's top-down approach. Similarly, such a theology says that for development to be genuinely beneficial to the people, it must be rooted in the socio-cultural soils where people live. It cannot start from the top, but must begin at the bottom.

The young African theologians recognize that theology in Africa loses its relevancy when removed from the cultural reality of a people and society. Globalization has not only weakened the nation-state but also the social and cultural constructs in which African theology is rooted. Theology in Africa has to rediscover the positive attributes of our culture and the pride of *ubuntu* for it to be able to fight globalization. Only through addressing some of Africa's fundamental cultural values can the continent hope to stand against outside forces. Marginalization of the youth, women, children, the disabled and other disadvantaged social groups has been seen as a major socio-cultural problem that needs to be addressed if society is to be empowered to stand as one against the negative effects of globalization, and to achieve meaningful development.

The dependency syndrome

It is generally accepted that Africans are worse off economically today than they were at independence. This is true both in absolute as well as in relative terms. Nigeria is perhaps the most dramatic example where the per capita income dropped from US$1,200 in 1983 to US$250 in 1995. Most other countries have fared just as badly save for Botswana, Mauritius and perhaps Gabon. During the 1980s, Africa's real GNP per capita declined 0.7 percent, while the average for the third world increased by 2.7 percent. For all of sub-

Saharan Africa, real income per capita dropped by 14.6 percent from its levels in 1965, making the people of that region worse off than they were at independence (UNDP world report).

After two decades of development work in Africa, the average African household has less food at the table (or rather, on the mat), fewer and poorer quality health services, less to spend on the education of children, no rural agricultural extension services and lower value for their cash crop. One could go on and on.

Africa is now a continent which cannot feed itself, meet its external financial obligations or the bill for its essential imports, protect its population, prevent environmental degradation, or exert any meaningful influence in the international decision-making processes. A number of African countries are now in danger of national disintegration, including some which, as recently as the 1980s, were held up as success stories.

The dependency syndrome relates to the fact that many local churches and NGOs depend on outside financing for almost all their funding. In most cases a withdrawal of external financing means, thus, the end of the NGO and its projects. One way out of the dependency syndrome is to provide a mechanism by which part of the funding for NGOs from outside may be used to build up an investment capacity for the local NGOs. Most international agencies, however, are reluctant to provide funds for capital development. Mwalimu Musheshe sees the reluctance of Northern NGOs to provide capital for investment as one of the reasons why there is need to rethink and reassess the relationship between African NGOs and those from the North.

The assessment, according to Musheshe, must involve a fundamental questioning of the African sense of worth and the need to question the sincerity of Northern NGOs in their commitment to the betterment of African lives. In essence, he sees the current development paradigm as no different from the top-down approach which characterized the modernization approach of the 1950s and 1960s and that of the international financial institutions in the 1980s and 1990s. The only difference here is that Northern NGOs have a "politically correct" ideology of grassroots development. Musheshe therefore calls for local empowerment that shows results, not rhetoric.

Are our discussions on this critical issue best served by this approach? Should we not pose the question differently, especially if we want to look into the future? How do we deal with the contemporary African predicament, and the human condition of the African people? How do Africans view themselves at this historical juncture? How does the rest of the world view Africa at Africa's most vulnerable moment? Such questions are provoked by the lead article in *The Economist* of 13-19 May 2000. The editorial comment titled "Hopeless Africa" concludes, "At the dawn of the 21st century Africa's experience is that of failure and despair as symbolized by Sierra Leone." The detailed lead article, in a very cynical way, goes on to paint the most pathetic picture of "The Hopeless Continent".

It is not the "facts" that concern us so much as the spirit of the article. In my view, the attitude of the writer of this article is that of a man who goes and sees a beautiful woman, rapes her and thereafter does everything to blame the victim for her condition. While the author of the article might see the continent as hopeless, Africans view it differently.

Even Sierra Leonians have not lost hope. Zainab Bangura, the director of the Campaign for Good Governance (Sierra Leone's leading NGO) might have given up all hope during her life in exile in Ghana. There, she had time to reflect on the destruction of her country and the devastation of the economy and the society by the protracted civil war. But she also reflected on the beauty of many Sierra Leonians, and especially the young people. She thought "how God must have had hope for us when he gave us the diamonds, gold, titanium, iron, cocoa, coffee, ginger and palm oil". There is no denying that the civil war in Sierra Leone was fuelled by the diamonds and other minerals. But that should not mean that the future is closed to those determined to change the prevailing conditions. As she prepared to return to Sierra Leone to build a new future, Bangura reasoned that "despite all these, there is a new sense of hope for the future... I feel a new sense of commitment, determination to join the many forces that are now struggling to ensure Sierra Leone sinks no further."

It is the resilience and determination of Africans like Bangura that show there is courage to hope even in the midst of what appears to *The Economist* as a hopeless situation. Failure there might have been, but not despair so far as many Africans are concerned. As long as Africans are prepared to reconstruct and rebuild the continent, there will always be the hope that life in Africa will be better – if not for us, then for the younger generation.

The dialectic of despair and hope

The Economist article poses a direct challenge to the experience with the WCC Harare assembly, which talked of "the journey of hope for Africa". At the assembly, the African participants reminded themselves of their difficult past, yet also rejoiced at their inspiration drawn from "the signs of hope such as the increasing acceptance of democratic governance, the end of the apartheid regime, and the Truth and Reconciliation Commission of South Africa" (the Harare covenant). It is clear that there is a dialectic between the two perceptions of seemingly the same reality. How does the ecumenical movement, as a strong advocate of development, respond to the human condition of the African people in the 21st century? We must continue to raise some questions that underlie what appears to be "the enduring paradox of aid".

Why is the African so poor while Africa is so rich? Why is Africa less developed after so much development work over such a long period of time? Why has aid to Africa (over US$400 billion since the 1960s) left the continent worse off than before? Such an amount of money could have funded no less than four Marshall plans. Why are Africans, who are said to love life so much, so busy killing each other? What happened to the relations of affection that characterize African daily life?

While local churches and NGOs are effective with respect to micro-projects, they do not have the capacity to manage large and complex programmes. They cannot, nor is it really their mandate to, establish infrastructure. That is the responsibility of the state, but it is one the state has long since abandoned. Yet, without good infrastructure, humanitarian and development work can only go so far and can be very frustrating. Should the development agencies continue the work despite their clear limitations? The flip side of the dilemma is another ethical question: Should we delay our development work until the infrastructure is in place, even if such a delay means denying the people their right to services?

Strong institutions and infrastructure are a prerequisite for sustainability in any development work. Without institutions, we might as well be planning to fail. Yet the ecumenical agencies do not fund institution-building, either as a matter of policy or because their mandate does not allow them. How then is the ecumenical movement expected to make an impact in the economic and social transformation in Africa?

Building self-confidence and living a life of dignity are considered essential elements in any meaningful development. Yet the very fact that development aid leads to the dependency syndrome severely undermines any chance of building self-confidence and maintaining dignity on the part of recipients. Should we still continue working with the same paradigm? What are the alternatives?

Our work is necessitated by the history of the last three centuries or so. Without the poor and the downtrodden, the funding agencies would have little reason to exist in their present nature and form. How should this realization inform and challenge the relationships between and among local and international NGOs, and between them and the people they serve?

If any level of sustainable transformation is to be achieved in Africa, it is imperative that social reconstruction shall characterize the journey of hope towards a better

Africa. Just as wholeness is essential for African community life, so also is our wider ecumenical community. We must envision reconstruction as we see all our relationships, in a holistic way. In order to move towards greater mutuality and genuine interdependence in the wider ecumenical community, perhaps we can begin to reconstruct patterns of relationship founded on wholeness with all it entails – justice, peace, righteousness – in the conviction that such God-given patterns of living will bring us closer to the promise of abundant life.

8. Ecumenical and Ethical Imperatives

If the third millennium will be the millennium of African Christianity for the world, succeeding the Euro-American and the Greco-Roman Christianity, it seems to me that it will not be the grand type of institutional forms of organized Christianity, neither will its ecumenism be hinged upon historical fragmentation of such institutions, but rather Christianity will thrive among organic communities living the moral traditions of abundant life. In other words the authentic future of the ecumenical movement will only be guaranteed by the growth and sustenance of dialogue and search for unity underlying the diversities among these communities in Africa.

Bénézet Bujo, *The Ethical Dimension of Community*

The agenda for the churches and the ecumenical movement in Africa has generally been responsive to the priorities and allocation of resources by the Northern agencies and churches. Hence, the very patterns of migration and bifurcation of the nation-state may be identified with trends and relations between the parent churches of the North and the local churches in the South. Such trends and patterns are ideologically driven with respect to allocation and access to resources, which are controlled and distributed by the churches and institutions of the North.

The ideologies of development in the earlier, post-colonial days influenced the theological self-understanding of the mission and calling of the ecumenical movement. Most projects were based on the philosophy of developmentalism and only much later, after the cold war, did it become fashionable to engage in advocacy, human rights and peace-oriented programmes. Furthermore, most projects ceased to be self-sustaining due to lack of foresight on the part of leadership and interdependency in relationships between local initiatives and international ecumenical agencies. An overview of contemporary trends is therefore vital if we are to explore the options and new frontiers of the ecumenical movement in Africa and the world.

The origin and nature of the ecumenical movement in Africa is characterized by particular responses to colonialism and the unceasing quest for unity within the family of the people of God. Institutional ecumenism in Africa was essentially formed and informed by insights gained in the Student Christian Movement and the World Council of Churches (WCC), and it was also influenced by the emergence of various processes and initiatives based on the spirit of pan-Africanism and the Bandung conference. (The Bandung conference in Indonesia in 1956 greatly influenced the formation of the non-alignment movement. Regional ecumenical organizations, especially the All Africa Conference of Churches [AACC] and the Christian Conference of Asia [CCA], were informed by the logic of the non-alignment movement.) The consolidation of the forces of self-determination eventually led to institutionalization of the original vision of political and ecumenical unity (i.e., Organization of African Unity and AACC) on the continent.

Yet the vision of unity articulated in political terms has never found a home-grown theological correlation. Neither have the institutional forms of ecumenism "from above" entered into adequate dialogue with the less structured and more people-driven forms of ecumenism from below. African cultural resources and cosmology which would provide a rich ground for dialogue and communion between the great religious movements and traditions of sapience, including Islam and Judaism, have largely been ignored.

Moratorium and self-reliance

The enduring dependency of local church and ecumenical institutions on external donor support from Western churches and state-linked institutions has re-energized the debate on self-governance and local ecumenical autonomy. During the AACC conference in 1974 in Lusaka, for example, the issue of a moratorium on external funding was high on the agenda. Burgess Carr, then AACC general secretary, called for the declaration of a moratorium on foreign missionaries and foreign funding of ecumenical and church work in Africa. Well aware of the risk involved, since AACC fully depended on Western donor support for all its work, Carr saw a moratorium as a cleansing hyssop, "a solid detergent capable of getting rid of certain dishonest and immoral practices which have distorted the mission of the church in Africa" in the words of Efiong Utuk. What motivated Carr was his genuine desire for dignity to be earned through self-reliance. John Gatu fully supported the call for moratorium. His own famous statement "missionaries go home" led him to found *jitegemea* (Swahili for "self-reliant") in the Presbyterian Church of East Africa of which he was the general secretary. *Jitegemea* has had some measure of success given that today the PCEA is perhaps the most self-reliant church in the region in so far as meeting basic budgetary obligations.

The moratorium required a theological equivalent to the *ujamaa* political philosophy of self-reliance in order to transform itself into an African spiritual movement of self-determination. Otherwise, it could have remained a simple slogan of insulation from dependency on grants from the Western donor agencies. Nevertheless, one may contend that, given the economic hardships of the mid-1970s owing to the oil crisis and especially due to lack of sustained local commitment to the declaration, the implementation of the moratorium became impossible. In the 1980s, African churches again became more dependent on their ecumenical partners abroad, and from 1990 there has been a steady decline of donations to churches and ecumenical institutions in Africa.

From the mid-1980s, the national councils of churches have participated in a different type of relationship with the ecumenical partners in affluent nations. This has been based on the principle of witnessing together in the struggle for life and striving for sustainable communities. Here, the ecumenical organizations in Africa host the annual "partners round table" consultations to share with others the problems and prospects of Christian ministry in their respective countries, and to explain what support may be needed from the other partners. The value and socio-economic impact of the round-table approach are yet to be fully assessed.

Previously in Abidjan, a few years after its formation, the AACC acknowledged that it had paid more attention to its relations with the West than with the African constituency.

Churches, too, continued to be divided along francophone, anglophone and lusophone lines. The fragmenting effects of foreign linguistic boundaries have remained an impediment to the growth of the ecumenical movement in Africa. Little study has been initiated at the level of continental ecumenism on how diversity of linguistic traditions in the continent itself may help foster greater unity and dialogue. The distinctive contribution of locally instituted African churches to the possibilities of celebrating linguistic diversities are yet to be appreciated. Language, both as the expression of the gift of diversity at Pentecost and as the basic human resource for proclaiming the kingdom of God, is one of the critical contributions of Africa to world Christianity.

The triple heritage (African, Arabic and European spirituality) of the African people and the gradual modernization of the continent have inculcated more complex forms of multiple identities than seem to exist anywhere else in the world. But due to the impact of globalization on local cultures, it has been virtually impossible to evaluate the level of influence these multiple identities have, especially on the younger generation of Africans. Nor has it been easy to predict how diversity is likely to influence the future of the continent.

The institutional claims of unity or search for unity are constantly questioned because of the lack of immediate and adequate preventive responses to the unceasing conflicts on the continent. Indigenous modes of consensus-building and moral authority are often left out in the search for lasting solutions to the problems related to the nation-state in Africa.

The formation, processes and significance of the modern state were not congenial to the values and norms of African communal societies. The European mentality which is the product of the struggles and eventual maturation of a system of capital accumulation could not successfully be assimilated into the ethical domain of asocial sociability in pre-colonial African communal systems of governance. The positive growth and development of the modern nation-state required the emancipation of the public sphere from the control and monopoly of the internal feudal and imperial regimes. The ethical basis for the emergence and development of the nation-state in Africa would require critical dialogue with the internal patrimonial systems and structures that undermine democracy.

With the end of official apartheid in South Africa as clearly marking the end of an era for institutions associated with pan-Africanism and internal self-determination, a creative exit from the euphoria of liberation and a clear entry into analysis of ground for alternatives is urgent indeed. This is symbolized by the historic gesture and ideological shifts within the Organization of African Unity. While the transition of OAU to African Union (AU) has not been adequately heralded as a major step towards Kwame Nkrumah's original vision of a United Africa, it certainly signifies an effort in the direction of consolidated regional cooperation which cannot be ignored by the AACC. The search for unity within the sphere of faith cannot ignore these major political developments, however frustrated or illusive they may seem. Institutional ecumenism will not survive without the reading of the signs of the times and translation of such insights into Christian witness coupled with a genuine search for economic self-reliance.

A new ecumenical vision

The emergence and growth of sub-regional ecumenical bodies such as the Fellowship of Councils of Churches in Southern Africa (Foccisa), the Fellowship of Councils and Churches in West Africa (Fecciwa) and the Fellowship of Councils and Churches in Great Lakes and Horn of Africa (Fecclaha) are a good sign of renewal and consolidation of regional partnerships around new ecumenical frontiers that bring closer to home the search for unity, peace and justice. These regional ecumenical bodies may provide a new model for regional consolidation with linkages and structures complementary to the continental body, the AACC. In so doing, there will be an alternative paradigm of institutional ecumenism unique to Africa that is not based on competition for diminishing resources from the North but rather on the local renewal of commitment to unity in the household of God.

The new vision of the ecumenical movement in Africa would certainly contribute new positive energies to the initiative being undertaken in the transition of the Organization of African Unity to the African Union. It should be a vision that promotes the discernment of new meaning of boundaries that transcends the colonial policy of divide and rule. By facilitating interaction, the ecumenical movement would enhance regional cocorporation in trade and industry. The movement of peoples and ideas from the east coast through central to west Africa and southern Africa is key in the reconstruction of Africa and must remain an active ecumenical agenda in the years ahead.

Ecumenical unity is not possible without a language of diversity genuinely grounded in the desire for unity. The various languages of the African people must be in dialogue beyond the colonial identity motifs and parts of nation-states which they tend to represent. There is need for a new language of ecumenicity based on the ordinary experiences and struggles of the African people.

Although much has been achieved in terms of high profile advocacy through ecumenical initiatives, especially in the case of eastern and southern Africa, the ecumenical movement has yet to provide much-needed leadership in the theological understanding of advocacy and translation of such understanding into the life of the church. While identifying positively with the progressive forces of change and occasionally extending ecumenical hospitality to civil society and political parties fighting for justice, the church must not lose touch with the common ground of its own identity.

In the absence of a creative exit from the contemporary general crisis of governance in Africa, there is a tendency even within the ecumenical movement to focus on the survival of national councils of churches as institutions. While it has been fashionable to initiate policy reforms, most regional and local ecumenical institutions have not been able to explore local alternatives, options and models of self-governance.

There are hardly any sites of ongoing critical self-reflection on possibilities beyond or outside the social options being offered by the market economy. The triumph of the market and the ideological fatigue experienced in the public sphere has encroached deeply on the heart of most progressive institutions, including the ecumenical movement, that only fresh thinking concerning alternative leadership and a well-informed citizenry will make a difference in Africa. The crisis of legitimacy in the ecumenical movement will worsen unless it begins to identify with the struggles for alternatives. So long as the ecumenical space for critical reflection is constricted, the institutional forms of ecumenism in Africa will become like the proverbial salt which has lost its taste.

One of the immediate and urgent questions now is how to harness local and global resources to strengthen the capacities of Christian communities to alleviate human suffering brought about by the HIV/AIDS pandemic and the poverty generated by structural adjustment programmes. How shall we rebuild confidence, regain dignity and reclaim integrity, and thus make hope a reality today and not just in some far distant and unknown future? The various initiatives of the World Council of Churches culminating with the eighth assembly in Harare have been a testimony that Africa is not alone in her journey of hope towards an alternative vision of life not just for herself but for the rest of the world.

Church traditions in Africa

The churches in Africa, as elsewhere in the world, are inspired by a self-understanding that their origins are found in God. They often perceive themselves to be the pilgrims and instruments of hope. This self-assessment varies from church to church, depending on the historical tradition and its relationship with the society.

On the one hand, there are the churches that owe their rise to Western Christianity, among them being the established mainstream institutions which sprang up from missionary activity. They have relatively well-educated clergy. One may describe their life-style and values as those of the mainstream middle class of an emerging African civil society. Many of the clergy from mainstream church institutions tend to be ecumenically oriented but are not adequately equipped beyond class consciousness since they share the ideological location of their urban elite counterparts in the civil service.

The working structures of these churches are usually modelled on those of their "mother churches" in the West. Besides modern methods of evangelism, the social component of the gospel is usually taken seriously by setting up development projects. Some of these churches, for instance, commit themselves to socio-political and human-rights issues. They often clash with their governments on the questions of abuse of power and how to achieve fairness in the distribution of national resources. But involvement in political rhetoric of *otherness* without an adequate alternative seems counter-productive. Beyond quoting biblical passages that justify the church's calling to advocacy, it is necessary that a coherent theological self-understanding of its mandate is well articulated and understood by the membership. Historically, however, most of these churches were allied to colonial governments and some, like the Anglican church, held the flag of the colonial government in one hand and the Bible in the other, notwithstanding support within the church for the struggle for freedom and self-determination.

On the other hand, there are the African Instituted Churches (AICs), which were established by African prophets and prophetesses. Many of these churches broke off from the original *historical* churches. In contrast to the established churches, a majority of AICs have neither an elite clergy nor well-functioning infrastructures or bureaucracy. They have simple liturgies that are linked to the earth, and leadership structures that emerged from African traditions. The original AICs were a movement against spiritual imperialism. Their services do not necessarily have to be conducted in churches or cathedrals, but are often held in the open and under trees. In most liturgies, nature is symbolized as a sacrament of God's presence. Some have developed syncretistic theologies that attempt to harmonize the cultural world-view of African society with the values of the gospel. Most of these churches are not in a position to deal with issues affecting Christians in Africa because they lack the institutional means to do so. Although they wave the banner of Christian authenticity, they often ignore the social component of the gospel.

The other category of churches can be classified under the evangelical or Pentecostal movements whose origin dates back to the "resurrection movement" of the West, particularly in the United States. These churches or "crusades", as some of them identify themselves, which raided Africa in the 1970s and 1980s, mainly preach individual and personal salvation. The socio-political component is not important to them. They support the status quo and praise capitalism. They produce apocalyptic literature and use "pop-liturgies" which are very attractive to young people. In the recent past, many members of the established churches have defected and joined them. These Pentecostal churches constitute a serious challenge to the prophetic mission and activities of the church in Africa. They are the fastest growing among Christian denominations and some of their forms of worship are a big attraction to youth. Their entrepreneurial approach to the gospel also appeals to the young and upcoming African professionals.

The Ethiopian and Egyptian Orthodox churches, which are just as old as anything in Christendom, must not be forgotten. They have a rich spiritual legacy which dates back to biblical times and emerged from contacts with other cultures over many centuries. Christianity in Africa is so full of vitality and charisma that the numerous new theologies of life and the varied interpretations of the gospel can hardly confine it.

The third church

In his books, *The Coming of the Third Church* (1978), *The Mission on Trial* (1979) and *The Chosen Peoples* (1982), Walbert Buhlmann deals with the overwhelming issue of the "third church". By the year 1980, there were over 200 million Christians in Africa. This number increases annually by 4.5 percent, and in some parts of Africa the rate of growth is as high as 10 percent. It was estimated that by the year 2000 there would be 350 million Christians in Africa – more than on any other continent. It is known that the largest and currently most expensive church building is in Africa, the Roman Catholic cathedral in Yomoussoukro, Ivory Coast – a controversial gift of Felix Houphouet-Boigny, then head of state, to the Roman Catholic pope in Rome.

Beyond numerical contents and visible structures, what does the future of Christianity hold for Africa and the world? The colonial transfer and migration of Christianity must be questioned yet again to unlock the underlying assumptions upon which the foundations and formulations of institutional meaning of being church are anchored.

It should never be forgotten that Christianity came to Africa in a colonial package, even if the heroic deeds of the early missionaries are to be praised. The partitioning that was done by the colonial regimes was further encouraged by the mission. Long before the arrival of Christianity, there were indigenous religious practices which preached a healing message embodied in nature. Of course, there were also different sub-cultures in Africa which had developed their own political structures and handled their own affairs. In so doing, however, they did not pursue a religious-expansionist policy. What the early missionaries wanted to achieve with the Good News actually resulted in the bad news of a bifurcated church. The mission brought cultural isolation and the legacy of ethnic subjectivity that still exist today in Africa. We should not close our eyes and fail to see that bureaucratization of power is the living reality of church governance in most churches in Africa. Even theological reflection is predicated upon structures of authority that no longer make sense given the resources that are available on the continent.

A critical question ought to be asked again: Must churches in Africa have the same structures as those of their European partners when it is practically financially impossible to uphold them locally? Of course, Western theology and that way of thinking have influenced the churches in Africa. Western influences on structures, liturgies and architecture are still very strong locally and the advancement in the process of Africanization and the search for an independent Christian identity remains a potential pitfall of anthropological theology, also known as inculturation. This is not a healthy starting point for a process of maturity in the established churches of Africa.

Church and state

Some church leaders in Africa, as elsewhere in the world, are faced with the theological dilemma of how to confront abuse of power without appearing to be disloyal to the state authority, especially where the church is directly and formally related to the state. Very often these church leaders are reminded (and some remind themselves) of Romans 13 and Paul's warning that they have a duty to obey the rulers. Many genuinely want to be loyal, but there is the question of whether it is morally right to be loyal to tyrants.

When any given human authority is no longer accountable to its constituency, then it loses the moral imperative for its existence. Disobedience to tyranny is an appeal to a higher moral authority, namely justice. The integrity of authority as a gift to society is intrinsic to the establishment of a just and peaceful social order. So the loyalty enjoined in Romans 13 may be seen as obedience to the harmony inherent in the systems and structures of self-governance.

In interpreting Romans 13, we cannot avoid dealing with some theological and ethical ambiguities. Is obedience to human authority submission to the inevitable demands of unlimited power or rather an exercise in just relationships between the led and the leader? Can the church claim to lead in the sphere of human conscience if it cannot accept the discipline of being led in matters of human governance? How are we to promote theological self-understanding of the church as a community of critical discernment and critical participation in social and political processes? Is the prophetic tradition in conflict with the basic tenets of civility? How can the church engage in political change while avoiding political co-option?

These issues point to the question of whether and how churches should build alliances with institutions of the civil society or even with opposition political parties to bring pressure to bear on the powers that be. What is clear is that the church cannot be involved in the direct politics of power transfer, i.e., the very crude stuff of *Realpolitik* games which is often guided by self-serving intrigues and the blind use of force. Neither could it be drawn into internal political arrangements of the parties involved, especially in the event of an election. The church's intervention in political crises ought to be focused beyond intra-party or state politics as defined by the notions of power transfer. However, critical solidarity with the voiceless remains paramount, as does the church's unceasing adherence to ethical responsibility as a custodian of social justice.

We have presupposed critical distance from partisan politics and a renewed articulation of the value of human life. In the eyes of God, how do we maintain credibility when churches advocate for democratic change in the political realm while they continue to retain structures and decision-making processes that are not, and are not seen to be, democratic? This reminds us of the maxim "charity begins at home". The internal power arrangements within church institutions are in themselves an impediment to the growth of good governance in the wider society. The appeal of secular corporate structures has led (sometimes misled) to the idea of bureaucratic systems that are more efficient in the delivery of products. Churches, especially in Africa, in an effort to adopt to modern management regimes, have appropriated systems and structures that are in themselves alienating and not supportive of life in the African community.

With regard to the question of democracy, the conflictual dimensions of Western dialectical systems can inflame and deepen the ethnic disparities within church membership. The idea of inclusivity and holistic participation is critical to the quality of prophetic witness to political leaders by churches in Africa. This must go beyond structural changes in internal governance; it must involve deep commitment and ethical responsibility on the part of church leaders. The churches must learn how to advocate for immediate political change while promoting a culture of participation. Building a culture of participation is a long and slow process, but there could be urgent need for particular, immediate changes. The ecclesial institutions ought to build partnership with the other civil society groups, social movements and political parties with regard to immediate constitutional and legal reform processes.

Assisting change through democratic and non-violent means is part of the prophetic mandate of the churches. This demands dialogue even with non-Christian agencies. Putting in place systems that would guarantee free and fair elections, establishing mechanisms of accountability in the exercise of power, and creating an environment of peaceful transfer of power is all part of this mandate. The churches together must openly denounce corruption and educate the electorate on participatory democracy in addition to social justice.

Very often, church leaders have to come to terms with their denominational or ethnic identity before they can act ecumenically or nationally. The tendency is to tilt conveniently towards ethnicity in times of serious crisis. The nation-state itself, as already demonstrated, is in a crisis by virtue of the ethnic question. The churches should take this question very seriously. How do the internal power arrangements signify ethnic stratification? This is a very deep question. The future work of the church should put the highest value on the human dignity of all the people, regardless of their station in life. Human dignity is to be understood as the bond that ties together the various categories of human and community rights.

The global and the local
How do initiatives of a spiritual nature translate into movements of resistance against forces of globalization and

reawaken the use of a community's cultural and intellectual resources for the empowerment of local people? Where do we find the nexus between the global and the local? There is dire need for new models of self-governing institutions that are anchored in the life experiences and traditions of the people.

The communitarian vision of discerning anew and building up local markets that reflect authentic economic needs is integral to achieving self-reliance. Economic globalization fragments local economies and kills local economic initiatives in Africa. The challenge of how to deal with this reality requires ecumenical accompaniment because it is too heavy a burden for African churches to bear alone.

We need to reappropriate the idea of Sokoni as a sacred space, not to be transgressed or subjected to forces of commodification, because it is the site of affirmation of life. There is a need for boundaries that clearly redefine the space available for self-determination and resilience. The ongoing privatization of sacred space leads to alienation of the community and peoples' connection with the ecosystem. Swamps, forests, rivers, mountains and the plains were all sacred sites (i.e., sites dedicated to life) once upon a time, and hence are part of the heritage and historical memory of African communities. The notion of wealth must be reinterpreted. Wealth ought to be understood as intrinsic to the value of life itself in such a way that there are aspects of wealth that are not subject to monetary value. Discernment of life in these terms helps us to value life itself and the dignity of humanity. In sharing life with life, the encounter with the other becomes a source of empowerment and not alienation.

The church in Africa must develop new structures and redefine its involvement in public affairs. For many Christians today, the gigantic church buildings are financial burdens that are now being questioned in view of the rampant poverty, inflation, unemployment, civil wars and increasing numbers of refugees in many African countries. Africa needs a church of the people that resembles the model of grassroot congregations in basic communities. These would be the congregations that are involved in social affairs and would create conditions in which people not only develop their theology but also practise it. They promote an ecumenical body founded at the grassroot level, rather than the institutionalized one that is established from the top. What is badly needed is the ecumenism of the heart.

Another model in the development of a church of the people is found in the encouragement and support of lay movements that are already ecumenical in their structure. Such movements could provide a forum for critical reflection on the future of the church in Africa. The first step towards renewing African Christianity should be the recognition of the valuable elements of African culture. The nightmare of divided spiritual loyalties cannot be overcome by establishing national church councils that provide nothing more than financial support for the many churches in Africa. There needs to be discussions and exchange on critical questions about society, the church and theology. The late Aaron Tolen, a political scientist and lay theologian from Cameroon, once raised the following disturbing questions:

> In almost every country, the democratization process is stalled by a denial of the right to dissent, dialogue, and ignorance of the common good. Can our churches, our councils of churches pretend to be models? Which country can pretend to be aloof from the tragedy going on in Rwanda, Burundi, Nigeria, Angola and Liberia? Christians, churches and councils of churches have seen all these tragedies emerge... What have we done?

In J.N.K. Mugambi ed., *Democracy and Development in Africa*, p.74

Tolen went on to argue that Christians, churches and church councils in Africa foresaw many disasters and were challenged to at least try to do something that could have stopped them. He laments that the churches did very little and for the most part kept silent. Consequently, he concludes,

> In Rwanda, the churches and the cathedrals are no longer safe places. One can get killed there just as in any other place. Being a priest, a pastor, a bishop or an archbishop has not made you a

different citizen and does not make you different from those who went out of control. We are all sitting in the same boat, but with one difference: we knew what was happening. We had the means to protest in order to divert the events to another direction. But we did not do our duty and failed in our role as watch-dogs.

All this goes to underline the point that even the church is not free from ethnic divisions. Today, many Christians want to have their "own bishops", which means somebody from their own ethnic community. Bishops simply have to be "sons of the home soil". This expression, that can be heard in many dioceses, shows that in many places bishops are considered to belong to the "wrong" ethnic group.

Such thinking along ethnic lines hampers effective evangelism; it also challenges the churches to rethink. Since most of the fragmenting and divisive forces were unleashed by the coming into being of a divided church, the churches have the historical burden to deconstruct ethnicity and rebuild Christian communities. Beyond institutional fragmentation, families have been separated and even divided by the rampant growth of denominationalism. Studies are yet to be undertaken on how the bifurcation of the state (see p.46) is parallel to the growth of syncretism, the latter being the creative manipulation of local cultural resources and Western expressions of Christianity and the former being the result of the incomplete establishment of the nation-state in Africa. The growth of tribal churches and semi-ethnic groupings is rather disturbing.

There can never be an ecumenical movement without the church. Broad-based ecumenism presupposes church bodies that are mature and inclusive in structure. If ethnic prestige is the sole factor in membership, then the ecumenical basis for relationship and dialogue is limited indeed. If power in terms of resources becomes the driving force of identity, then the basis for ecumenical dialogue remains superficial. With the advent of globalization that has led to greater fragmentation of neighbourhood communities, the task to rebuild relationships between institutions and peoples is urgent. The challenge is to localize ecumenical expressions of solidarity by building relationships or creating new spaces through which new communities may emerge. The national councils of churches should become sites of rebuilding communities through untiring dialogue and self-reflection aimed at inspiring new thinking.

The way in which the church in Africa handles the issue of rebuilding communities will show whether it has passed the test of maturity. The fight against ethnic discrimination even within the church itself is an important prerequisite for an effective evangelism. No help from outside, whatever the organization, can sow the spirit of love and forgiveness among the Tutsi and Hutu in Rwanda, and no considerable financial aid or external involvement can create peace in Africa, so long as there is neither the atmosphere nor the environment in which this peace can be realized.

Ecumenical initiatives in advocating for justice and reconciliation can be difficult in situations where the church's prophetic ministry might have had a low priority in the past. The National Council of Churches in Kenya (NCCK) tried to create a forum for solving ethnic conflicts in Kenya in the early 1990s. However, because the church council had played a rather passive role in the 1960s and 1970s during the controversy surrounding the repossession of land, it was very difficult to create a neutral forum for solving disputes. When people ask where the church was during the massacre in Rwanda, the answer reads in part: some of the murderers were members of the church!

Democratization

The new role of the church in the process of democratization is a sign of its vital presence in Africa. For the first time in Zambia, for example, the church exercised a critical social responsibility in the 1991 general elections.

During the first free elections in South Africa in April 1994, the South African Council of Churches (SACC) alongside the Episcopal Conference of Catholic Bishops participated in the Ecumenical Monitoring Programme on South

Africa (EMPSA), initiated and internationally coordinated by the WCC. EMPSA election-observers were distributed in different polling stations in South Africa to monitor the polling proceedings in different regions, from the logistical requirements on the ground to the reporting of any irregularities. Shortly afterwards, in May 1994, there were also elections in Malawi. The church, supported by an ecumenical team of observers, also played a key role there.

The NCCK and the SACC have recently paid attention to questions on Christian ethics in African politics, with some success. The churches were committed to their role in society and wanted to contribute towards creating conditions under which people would utilize their freedom in a responsible manner and strive to live in dignity. As an institution, the churches in South Africa (the South African Council of Churches and the Catholic Bishops Conference) have remained in critical solidarity with the oppressed and suffering people. Owing to the change in South Africa, the church must learn to distance itself from a partisan involvement in politics. By creating the necessary space for good governance and sharpening the awareness of citizens, the church becomes God's advocate for change.

The origin of the demand for democracy is deeply rooted in African society. From the time Africa was swept by a wave of democracy early in 1990, which began with the national conference in Benin, the release of Mandela and the lifting of the ban on the African National Congress (ANC), the number of democratic regimes has risen sharply.

Although Africa joined the global democratic revolution relatively late, it is now at the forefront as far as change of regimes is concerned. According to statistics, thirteen of the countries that have been able to improve their level of freedom since 1991 are in Africa. In addition to the nine democracies and the liberal semi-democracy in Senegal, twenty or more countries south of the Sahara have been under pressure to embrace democratic changes.

This democratic wave was referred to as "the second liberation" because it promised to free the Africans from tyranny, oppression, corruption and bad political and economic systems which had dashed the hopes cherished at the first liberation in the 1960s.

A genuine democratization in Africa must surmount immense obstacles. The seriousness and honesty of many African heads of state is questionable. In far too many cases, autocrats of many years, such as Gnassingbe Eyadema in Togo, Paul Buja in Cameroun, Omar Bongo in Gabon, Daniel arap Moi in Kenya and Albert Réné in Seychelles consented to some kind of democratic elections, but there was no absolute freedom of the press, respect for the law, independence of the executive or other guarantees in place that are necessary for conducting free, fair and sensible elections.

Although free and fair elections are not an absolute guarantee of democracy, they are, nevertheless, a good indicator of how democratic a country is. As experiences in Zimbabwe (1980), Namibia (1990), Benin (1991) and Zambia (1991) have shown, international monitoring of elections can contribute to the strengthening of the integrity of the institutions responsible for the elections, the elimination of cheating and violence, the encouragement to participate in elections, the emphasis on the legality (both nationally and internationally) of the election process and the legitimacy of the election results.

However, the churches must not forget that the call for democracy does not concern only political regimes in Africa. Power is power, be it in governments, non-governmental organizations or churches. The churches can genuinely raise their voices in a changing world only if they also decisively reform the hierarchical and partly undemocratic leadership structures in their own houses. The growing influence of the civil society in Africa must lead to a comprehensive democratization in the state and in the society.

Ecumenism in Africa

The churches and the ecumenical movement in Africa must be in the vanguard in advocating a radical shift from institutional bureaucratization of power as a paradigm of social delivery to more interdependent, participatory models of governance. Strategies should be put in place to promote ecumenism from below and strengthen inter-religious dialogue between parish and mosque. The problem of programmatic frameworks and the contemporary institutional forms of ecumenism in Africa must be faced squarely. Are we on the verge of a major paradigmatic shift, or are we experiencing a looming crisis of corporate ecumenism?

Contemporary theological training and curricula in most church institutions do not seem to respond to the prevailing ideological and social consequences of global and local trends on the continent. Links between theoretical understanding of the mission and calling of the church and the realities facing the continent must be addressed and acted upon. High profile human-rights advocacy, peace-building initiatives and corporate imaging of ecumenical institutions seem to be the main sphere of public visibility.

To be able to engage meaningfully in emerging global trends, African churches must begin to initiate dialogue on alternatives to the triumph of the market-place and global corporate capitalism. They are challenged to imagine new forms of ecumenical movement as sites of synergy and nourishment for the emergence of life-giving communities, especially for the poor and the suffering in Africa.

The ecumenical community should provide leadership in the development of new methodologies of dialogue as preventive mechanisms against conflicts and war. Building institutions with ethical responsibilities will have to be an integral part of the ecumenical agenda. The churches must now set a new pace to reverse the trends of apathy and nihilism among youth and provide space for moral enthusiasm and courage to hope. It is by developing new schools of leadership and democracy as sites of learning that the churches will participate in the birth of new movements. The curriculum for this new learning will be fully informed by the moral traditions of abundant life in order to help avert the threat of social death in Africa. Alternative schools will be not only a market-place of new ideas for the future but the place where new communities of memory will reside. They will be places where people go to encounter dialogue and celebrate diversity as a gift of creation, not the occasion for conflict. We look forward to the growth of new forms of ecumenical witness in which communities are revived because of renewed hope.

Finally, the question of ecumenical relations hinges upon issues of access and sharing of resources. When resources become the defining instruments in ecumenical relations, the categorization of those who have the means to the goods and those who seek the goods becomes determinative. What are often referred to as horizontal relations of partnership actually become vertical relationships based on power and access to information. Any authentic relationship between partners must include dialogue on the structure of such relationships. If round-table conferences on how to allocate and administer resources for particular projects in the third world are to gain in meaning, they should engage the sociology of power around the table. Most communities and institutions in the South seeking support for public initiatives are trapped by their vulnerability to Western funding agencies. The very concept of donor/recipient relations is ethically unsound, so new language and discernment must be found. If proximity to resources is defined in terms of power, then it will be impossible to develop relationships based on mutuality.

Without the means to negotiate with dignity, ecumenical and secular institutions in Africa have been led to tailor their programmes to suit the policies of Northern agencies. These programmatic frameworks tend to reflect institutional survival mechanisms rather than homegrown initiatives. It is this factor that has contributed to the decadence and fragmentation of dependent institutions in Africa.

Without dignifying forms of mutual relationships, there has been a continual erosion of institutional confidence in Africa. This must stop if reconstruction of wholeness is a prerogative for ecumenical renewal in the continent. It is an open secret that the ecumenical community has given the secular world a new language and logos of paradigms that often are used to support other, problematic ways of acting. However, in this regard the ecumenical movement ought to provide not only the vocabulary but also the model of how to relate on the basis of partnership and mutual vulnerability. Resources must be subject to the norms of accountability, horizontal relations and management of the gifts of God for the people of God.

Ethical and spiritual discernment

The main challenge facing churches in Africa is the ability to develop capacities for ethical discernment, advocacy and programmes, which link processes at grassroots level where action is needed and to the national and regional levels where policy is formulated. The other challenge is how to channel common, concerted efforts ecumenically at the grassroots level in response to conflicts and human suffering within these communities. Churches must be equipped with the knowledge of contemporary links between global and local situations if they are to gain a clear understanding of the dilemmas Africa is facing and why. It is absolutely vital to carry out a *social audit* of the prevailing trends within civil society, donor agencies, political institutions and the private sector in Africa – not so much to excavate the facts and events but to relate the events taking place with a larger vision based on ethics and the primacy of non-market values of life.

The concept that the promise of abundant life provides a framework for ethical discernment should be explained as a basis of common action. Often, ecumenical institutions have been challenged to explain the rationale for their political involvement both to their own constituency (self-understanding) and to society. Three decades of non-involvement left the citizens in Africa ignorant of their civic rights as well as their civic responsibilities. The shift from developmentalism in the 1960, 1970s and 1980s to advocacy has made ethical identity central to the self-understanding of the ecumenical movement and the church in Africa.

The biggest challenge in the 21st century is to promote spiritual discernment as a basis for corporate life. As an integral part of ecumenical social responsibility, we shall educate the people about their rights and engage the public in a critical political and social audit. The tremendous achievements of the national councils of churches especially in eastern, southern and western Africa in accompanying democratic change in delicate political situations provide a useful ecumenical memory supportive of future struggles. Such achievements should be carefully documented.

The vocation to educate, sensitize and awaken local membership of the NCCs to their ethical and social responsibility is itself a call to engagement in the search for unity. What churches have been called to be and do in situations of gross violations of human rights is to affirm our ethical vision that claims every living being as part of the household of God. Human dignity is to be understood as demanding the restoration of the *imago Dei* in all human relations.

But the question of dignity is not exclusive to the realm of human experience. It also includes the institutions that mediate human experience. As already noted in chapter 6, part of the process of restoration of dignity is reconstruction of the legitimacy of the state, of social interventions and of leadership as prerequisites to the success of democracy (dignified participation in public policy processes) in Africa.

There are numerous biblical references and stories about individuals whom God called by their names: from Adam and Eve, Abraham, Sarah and Hagar, Moses and Samuel to prophets like Jeremiah and Nehemiah. Jesus also calls his disciples each by name, as well as other individuals like Mary, Martha and Lazarus. This calling of the individual by name signifies the worthiness of the person before God. By virtue of having been created, each individual has, independently of all others and all else, a relationship with God and vice versa. The criterion against which the worthiness of a person is to be measured is the image of God in every person, not some utilitarian criteria derived from the Enlightenment that modernity tries to impose. The human dignity of individual persons is to be understood in terms of the nature of the being, created by God, that is human.

This Christian vision of humanity is not to be confused with radical humanism, which defines the individual human person as the subject of understanding and will. In this humanistic understanding the worthiness of a person, the identity of the person and therefore the way the society has to treat him or her, is based on a material vision of human reality. Persons are viewed merely as materials that may be freed, exploited, oppressed or even dispensed with. Those of lesser qualities in the society are expendable. They are seen as objects whose lives are at the mercy of institutions and individuals with *higher qualities of being* – a kind of social Darwinism. Carried to its logical conclusion, radical humanism would have a hierarchical view of the claim for human and people's rights. In this view, the entitlement to human rights would be dependent upon the social status of the individuals. This conception of humanism strips the dignity from individuals and groups of individuals (communities) whom the society considers as materially weak or inferior.

It is imperative that our ethical discernment and action lead to caring and sustenance of life. Development of curricula based on theological reflection, in which secular instruments of social analysis are creatively integrated with the ethical foundations of biblical interpretation of events, is vital. Engaging social scientists and young theologians on the continent of Africa to create a variety of communities of critical reflection, in order to facilitate and articulate such ecumenical responses, will help to equip the churches to read and respond adequately to the signs of the times. The suffering and misery experienced in Africa today serves as an invitation to the vocation of restoration of a people's dignity and the sanctity of all life. It is an invitation to awaken the hearts and minds of Africa's people, the authentic hope for a new life of abundance and fulfilment.

9. Torments of Death and Rebirth of the Spirit

> It is now common knowledge that in HIV/AIDS it is not the condition itself that hurts most (because many other diseases and conditions lead to serious suffering and death), but the stigma and the possibility of rejection and discrimination, misunderstanding and loss of trust that HIV positive people have to deal with.
>
> Gideon Byamugisha, Nov. 2001

In this chapter, we make a case for affirmation of values, soul and spirit of African heritage in the face of death. Africa is currently ranked the leading continent in infections and death resulting from the HIV/AIDS pandemic. It has been estimated that gradual depopulation of Africa may eventually lead to the wiping out of whole sections of the society in a matter of decades. HIV/AIDS in sub-Saharan Africa is a plague of genocidal proportions. No other calamity since the slave trade has depopulated Africa at the rate AIDS is doing today.

The churches in Africa and the worldwide ecumenical movement affirm that the struggle against AIDS is today a top priority on the ecumenical agenda. The global consultation on ecumenical response to HIV/AIDS in Africa convened by the WCC in Nairobi, Kenya, in November 2001 put emphasis on prevention, care, training, counselling, treatment and advocacy. External support is welcome, but the greatest impact will depend on the commitment of the churches and ecumenical organizations within Africa itself. The African church itself will have to change language, policy, behaviour and mobilize its own resources to reverse the epidemiological trend and give hope to those infected and affected by HIV/AIDS.

The Ecumenical Advocacy Alliance (EAA) (based in Geneva, Switzerland), an initiative of ecumenical funding partners and the WCC, chose HIV/AIDS alongside economic justice as the two most pressing issues around which to do global advocacy. In choosing HIV/AIDS, EAA acknowledged the pandemic to be "one of the greatest health challenges facing the world at the moment. It is also, arguably, the greatest challenge to prospects of social and economic development and global security."

HIV/AIDS is not just a disease whose eradication depends on medical treatment and care. It is far more complex than that. It has political, economic and social dimensions, all of which must be addressed if the phenomenon is to be dealt with in its totality.

A panel of international scientists looking into the various controversies regarding the nature of HIV/AIDS and the toxicity of particular anti-retroviral drugs concluded that Africa has to deal with the following paradoxes – that, contrary to developments in the Western world, HIV/AIDS in Africa is basically heterosexually transmitted and that today, while relatively few people die of AIDS in the West, millions in Africa have no access to basic heath care, let alone anti-retroviral drugs. As cases of AIDS deaths are declining in other parts of the world, even greater numbers of Africans are destined to die. But one must take note of the fact that if the available information on the nature of the disease and the numerous scientific resources were to be insulated from the madness of the market, humankind would have found a lasting solution to the HIV/AIDS pandemic.

The most viable option, at least for those who have not yet contracted the virus, is vaccination. Concerted efforts are employed in research for an HIV vaccine. Yet some of these efforts are being undermined. Recently, local scientists and doctors in Kenya who were developing an HIV vaccine with Britain's Oxford university were excluded from patenting the discovery. Job Bwayo, then head of the Kenya AIDS Vaccine Initiative (KAVI), made it very clear: "Immediately we realized our names were not included, we entered into correspondence with our collaborators to ensure we were reflected as part of the researchers. We are waiting for the outcome."

The news came as a shock to many African scientists since the theory behind the development of the vaccine was motivated by the experience of prostitutes in Nairobi's Majengo slums. The latter were found to have killer-T cells in their systems that protected them from HIV infection. Using this knowledge, scientists at the University of Nairobi's department of microbiology and those from

Oxford developed a vaccine construct to stimulate the generation of such cells in other human beings. This initiative has come to be popularly known as KAVI. The initiative received KSh.709,800,000 ($9.1 million) from the International AIDS Vaccine Initiative (IAVI), an international NGO based in New York. The NGO is known to have been funding vaccine initiatives around the world, including in South Africa and Uganda, and has a joint agreement with Oxford University on patenting the vaccine.

Hypocrisy in the scientific world

The controversy surrounding the question of intellectual property rights with respect to research on HIV/AIDS reflects the degree of hypocrisy in the scientific world. However, neither the sex workers nor the local scientists have control over the legality of the research findings so far. While people are dying, Western pharmaceutical companies and research institutions are making millions of dollars due to patenting rights and deregulation of the global drug market. Only as recently as 2001 did the government of Kenya make a plea to purchase more than three hundred million condoms from foreign companies as a strategy to curb the spread of the disease. The controversy over the use of condoms is not just based on concern about sexual morality: rather, it is a question of who is benefiting from their manufacture and distribution.

During the AIDS conference in South Africa in 2001, there was major lobbying by private interest groups to de-link the HIV/AIDS pandemic from its social, economic and political locations which constitute the very fabric of the disease. In other words, behind the war of words at the international conference on HIV/AIDS is what I call instrumentalization of misery in the market.

While we live with very scary statistics when it comes to AIDS in Africa, it is even more alarming that, in some parts of the continent, diseases such as malaria kill more people than AIDS-related diseases. The AIDS industry is vast indeed – from those who do research and produce drugs; to those who supply condoms and those engaged in social entrepreneurial activities such as awareness-raising; to many quacks who have mushroomed, claiming to have found a cure; to the coffin industry and proliferating funeral homes in Africa. While it is a good idea for AIDS advocacy to be a central focus of the UNDP, it is nevertheless unfortunate to do it at the expense of relegating malaria (which is proven to kill over one million Africans a year) to a non-priority. UNDP director Mark Brown claims that "HIV/AIDS has a qualitatively different impact than [the] traditional health killers such as malaria. It rips across social structures, target-ing people, particularly girls. By cutting deep into all sectors of society, it undermines vital economic growth – perhaps reducing future national GDP size in Africa by a third over the next 20 years."

This is all well argued and indeed true, but one does not have to be a rocket scientist to know that malaria does exactly the same – "it rips across social structures... cutting deep into all sectors of society... and undermining economic growth". The only difference is that there are hardly any international NGOs distributing free mosquito nets supplied by USAID or the United Nations. Furthermore, there are many statistics being thrown around by just about everybody and so, while appreciating the depth of the scourge, some degree of sobriety especially with regard to Africa must be retained.

The most chilling nightmare concerning HIV/AIDS is the fact that it brings about a slow, gradual, painful process of death. Communities, families and individuals are helpless as they watch their own sons and daughters bound in hopeless-ness. The misery that comes with death leaves so many unan-swered questions in the minds and hearts of the bereaved. The calamity visits not just individuals but a whole range of persons related to the immediate victims. The cumulative effects of HIV/AIDS brings down productivity in national economies, demoralizes populations and leads to social nihilism. People give up living, and societies are engulfed by the fear of the unknown.

The African ethical framework implies that, for an individual to be, he or she is and must be seen to be part of an extended family or community. This understanding is the vital source of moral strength in managing disease. The outbreak of the AIDS pandemic is challenging Africans to rethink communitarian ethics. There is need for a responsible approach to sexuality whereby we go deeper and further than an isolated change of behaviour.

Stigmatization of human sexuality is not the solution. Worse still is the stigmatization and rejection of AIDS sufferers. There is the terrifying tendency among some churches to read into and even transform the whole phenomenon of HIV/AIDS into the apocalyptic event – God's curse upon humankind! – and to suggest that Africans are the perpetual bearers of this curse. Such simple mis-reading of calamities is dangerous and serves to alienate those living with the disease.

It is urgent that a new culture of understanding human sexuality be encouraged to evolve, whereby sexual encounter is seen from its communal dimensions instead of stressing only a one-dimensional and individual-oriented self-realization as the highest value. The indigenous ethics of human sexuality must be revisited. While sexual encounter is primarily between individuals, the outcomes have always had communal implications. A case in point is when the outcome is reproduction, or again in contracting any sexually transmitted disease, especially AIDS. In the latter case, the matter gains greater currency in case of sickness and or eventual death of the parties concerned. In either case, the community is involved.

But there is also a link to the global economic order in the spread of HIV/AIDS, which encourages illicit trading in drugs and recycling of dirty money, depriving the individual persons of dignity in the most brutal manner. Some very obvious examples from Africa include the legacy of apartheid-era bachelor hostels in South Africa, and today elsewhere on the continent, where workers are forced by economic hardships to live single lives in towns, leaving their spouses in the country. These situations will be greatly exacerbated by economic globalization.

We live in a world where even our sexuality has become a commodity. The tendency to treat sexuality as such leads to emphasis on technical advice which entails increased use of condoms while the moral admonition of individual faithfulness tends to alienate and locate the discourse outside one's immediate community. A new culture of sexuality based on the communitarian ethic must begin, raising questions of social and structural violence.

A theology of life in the context of the HIV/AIDS pandemic

The challenge of the HIV/AIDS pandemic requires a creative and well-thought out response by churches. Moreover, the churches together should facilitate communities in developing skills for accompanying those who are living with the reality of death. Communities of the resurrection, based on a profound theological understanding of the moral power of innocence, are vital indeed. The number of infected people is said to increase by 7000 persons per day including 1400 babies, which is accelerated by conditions of poverty and ignorance about the nature of the pandemic. Education and correct information, especially about preventive measures, are invaluable in reversing the trend of AIDS.

In HIV/AIDS, the tragedy is that the very means by which human life comes to being has become the source of death and raises the threat of non-being. We are called to transform this tragedy by linking life to a moral cosmology as the means to reclaim the intrinsic value of being in the world. That is why a new expression of the theology of life in the context of the HIV/AIDS pandemic would be liberating indeed.

The approach would be to identify and analyze the forces that sustain, protect, enhance and enrich life, compared to the forces that seek to destroy life. Themes of hope beyond the void, spiritual and ethical exposition on the meaning of life beyond death, using the ordinary languages of the people, would enrich the discourse on alternative ways of living with HIV/AIDS. The values of equanimity that knit the web of relations of kinship and community would enable people to experience collective resurrection in the face of death. The church is called to three vital areas of response – theology, ethics and pastoral care. The church must become for the ailing and dying children of Africa a place of solace and compassion, indeed a sanctuary of life.

The receding role of governments in providing basic health care and the growing involvement of the private and non-governmental sector in this regard demand an urgent response from the ecumenical movement in Africa. Nearly 55 percent of health-care service delivery is offered by the private sector while most mission hospitals have been taken over by governments. It is therefore urgent that an alternative institutional framework be established to meet pressing needs and consolidate the links between the socio-economic realities and health-care demand, especially for women in Africa. In situations where more than 50 percent of the population living below the poverty line are women (the feminization of poverty), there is need for affirmative action in health-delivery systems.

There are other dimensions of the crisis of health care in Africa that affect women, specifically in relation to violence. Contemporary medical training in most African countries does not equip trainees with skills for dealing with the consequences of domestic violence and other forms of violence, especially rape. Over the past ten years, domestic violence and its consequences have become a global public health issue.

The absence of clarity and links between public heath policy and human-rights advocacy has led to a crisis of response to the emerging health needs of women. The current health-care framework is unable to respond adequately to the socio-medical aspects of domestic violence, rape and emergency obstetric care. The situation is further aggravated by the absence of institutional response to this predicament. Due to the fact that public health-care systems have become dysfunctional and the cost of private health services is beyond the reach of a majority of the people in many African countries, it is critical that churches revive the traditional component of mission hospitals as part of the ministry of healing and wholeness.

The health-care situation is made worse by the erosion of communal social safety-net structures which guaranteed the security of widows, orphans and the poor in rural Africa. It is imperative that a wider, concerted ecumenical initiative be established for the continent to consolidate resources and accompany local communities in their struggles to bring new hope to the poor and the suffering.

The need for global partnership in facing the crisis of HIV/AIDS is critical indeed. But we must always return to the values and norms of experiences with living communities in Africa. The people of Africa have always cherished an integrated vision of social reality. It is this connection between human experience and the structures or systems that yields an integrated understanding of the value of life.

Thus the various belief systems and institutions of philosophy in Africa remind us that we live in a moral universe nurtured by the web of life-giving and sustaining relationships among all beings that inhabit the earth, including the ancestral spirits.

The human condition is at the heart of our experience of the universe, and it is held together not by dualistic systems or inanimate objects but by institutions of affection that guarantee human happiness. New methodologies and preventive measures against the spread of HIV/AIDS, especially among young people, are necessary. Building institutions with ethical responsibilities for moral life, especially in the midst of communities, is essential.

10. Ecuspace and the Sanctuary of Life

> Our existence as embodied being is purely momentary; what are a hundred years in eternity? But if we shatter the chains of egotism, and melt into the ocean of humanity, we share its dignity. To feel that we are something is to set up a barrier between God and ourselves; to cease feeling that we are something is to become one with God. A drop in the ocean partakes of the greatness of its parent, although it is unconscious of it. But it is dried up as soon as it enters upon an existence independent of the ocean. We do not exaggerate when we say that life is a mere bubble.
>
> Mahatma Gandhi's philosophy

This chapter considers the meaning and place of ecumenical solidarity and accompaniment of all who struggle in the 21st century. In the latter part of the 20th century, "solidarity" became a household word among peoples' movements and non-governmental organizations (NGOs) that sought to support those actively seeking liberation and social justice. For the ecumenical movement, sharing of resources was a concrete expression of solidarity with the poor and marginalized.

In the 21st century, sharing must be intensified and deepened in other ways; for the majority of the victims of economic globalization, life will be nothing but a long-drawn-out death. The earth is the sanctuary of life, and the household of God is sacred space; hence, one may allude to a cosmic ecumenicity of life. We share the space of life with all sentient and non-sentient beings. This is a given and not an imposed condition.

As we trail through a variety of thoughts, we shall begin by engaging certain distortions of the Jesus story and finish by unlocking the power of the story in relation to other stories of life. We shall explore the story of the historical Jesus according to a view of life based on African spirituality.

Christianity is the world's most widely inculturated religion because it is the most widely translated of all world religions. Inculturation refers to appropriation or internalization of values into a culture without necessarily distorting or destroying essential identity. In Christian theology, the term has been used to describe evangelization of culture from within. Thus, the Christian good news comes to people from within the perspective of their culture. This requires that the instruments of mission be built upon the resources of the culture of the people being evangelized.

But inculturation would be impossible were it not for the translatability of the Christian message itself and the receptivity of the culture in question. At the heart of the issue of translatability of the Good News is the message itself. The message of Christianity is essentially embodied in the translated historical reality of Jesus of Nazareth who neither left any recorded account of his teaching nor founded an organized religion.

It is this fact of historicity and the undefined nature of Christianity that helped it spread throughout the world by appropriating and being appropriated into every tongue, thought and conduct of a people. The inner logic of Christianity allows for creative participation of every human initiative in the quest for the ultimate truth and meaning of life. In this regard, we shall introduce the notion of ecumenical inculturation towards the end of the chapter, thereby proposing a new language of ecumenicity through the creative use of local cultural resources.

Philosophy and inculturation

Western dualistic visions of reality breed conflictual social organizational structures and an adversarial way of conducting public life. So we begin to explore the intricacies of Western dualism and the creation of otherness, seeking other options and alternatives outside the box. The quest for the historical Jesus, for example, in broad terms has largely been a process of reproduction of the cultural and intellectual values at particular moments of social anxiety in Europe. This anxiety was ignited with the crisis of legitimacy that the church was going through during the turbulent times of the Reformation. The sacred texts had been set free by Martin Luther's rebellion into the hands of ordinary people and intellectuals of his time. For the first time, the sacred scriptures became public documents. Henceforth, interpretation of biblical texts would be subjected to the social trends and rational inquiry of the day; in other words, religious discourse was to be deconstructed into the discourse of "common sense".

With the Reformation, the church was no longer seen as the ultimate authority, and its mandate was in doubt not only in matters of faith but also in governance and public life. Then there was the emergence of new philosophical movements that were greatly influenced by the new paradigm of empirical investigation. The burgeoning effects of Newtonian physics and the Cartesian principle of reason as preceding existence *(cogito ergo sum)*, and the influx of social upheavals, all were part of the realities of this period. Scientific methodology soon became the means of attaining certitude with respect to knowledge. An anxiety for authentic and reliable authority paved the way to epistemological scepticism. The new way of knowing the world by unknowing it had dawned upon Europe. Rational empiricism and positivism in Britain, idealism and phenomenology in continental Europe, and other closely related epistemological systems became part of the intellectual currency that drove reason beyond the boundaries of scientific inquiry.

There was also a spilling over of the industrial revolution, especially in Britain, with its contradictions that offered the perfect laboratory for the development of Karl Marx's brilliant tools of social analysis. This, of course, anticipated the post-modern component of ontological agnosticism. Some Marxist concepts, especially with regard to fetishes of commodities and human labour in relation to class stratification, also became part of the standard vocabulary in social discourse. Certainly these ideas migrated into the quest for the historical Jesus in very subtle ways – for example, the idea that the disciples were lazy and had nothing to do after the death of Jesus, and so they invented the resurrection in order to maintain a certain life-style of dependency. The Marxist notion of work also found its way into the Jesus project through the objectification of non-European civilizations.

The initial experiments in the quests for the historical Jesus first took place largely on the periphery of ideological constructs in Europe. But the nascent historiographical idea of fact as truth had also begun to influence the understanding of history. The objective reality of events was now being scrutinized on the basis of a new methodological doctrine – evidence. Things were said to have really happened because there is undoubted evidence that they really happened as reported or documented. They are quantifiable in empirical terms; i.e., information about their happening can be verified by independent sources.

So the underlying assumption among the Jesus seekers was that the gospels were historically accurate only where they were true "factual" accounts of the life and times of the man Jesus. They treated the gospels as if they were detailed biographical documentation of the life of Jesus. John Locke, the British rational empiricist, opened the gates of legitimate doubt concerning the sacred texts, raising questions if there was lack of evidence. To the degree that one could ascertain the miracles as evidence of divine providence, one could believe; however, in the absence of evidence one was no longer held accountable to faith. Responsibility for belief was based on various degrees of evidence. The texts were then open to scrutiny but, with religious upheavals still unsettled, one could not engage in an open public discourse about such scrutiny.

By reconstructing the life of Jesus using the available records (apart from the gospel of Thomas and the writings of Josephus, no major sources outside the official canon were available to provide an alternative frame of reference or critique), the early modern commentators exposed the apparent contradictions in various historical accounts and questioned the legitimacy of the canon in providing accurate accounts of the life of Jesus. In so doing, these authors questioned the interpretations of scripture given by the church. The texts were demystified and miracles became a source of ridicule so that Jesus was depicted sometimes as a trickster, a simple millennial prophet with a streak of secrecy, or a wandering sage whose mission was sometimes unknown even to himself.

Eurocentrism and biblical interpretation

With the discovery of the Dead Sea scrolls and the development of philological techniques, the study of the origins and literary forms of the scriptures become more and more sophisticated. Meanwhile, the quest for the historical Jesus had been interrupted. Herman Remairus, David Straus and Ernest Renan had earlier initiated this quest and were later followed by Albert Schweitzer. Though varied with strong nuances reflecting the intellectual climate of their own times, they all orientalized Jesus, objectifying him and making him a "toy" of the European cultural predicament in a world that was basically their playground.

This intellectual mischief among German scholars supplied the nations of Europe with necessary ideological tools for the colonial project. In 1884 and 1885 at the Berlin conference, while texts on the historical Jesus were being written, a divided Europe stood united against Africa. The colonial portrait of Jesus as the Christ of European culture supplied them with the moral justification to conquer or destroy with impunity other cultures and their economies.

Later, though Albert Schweitzer depicted a Jesus of pristine spirituality and charisma, Schweitzer's analysis of the ethic of work reduced Africans to lazy, acrobatic savages whom God delivered to be rescued by the hands of Europeans. Missionary activity for Schweitzer's generation was not just about spreading the message of Jesus; it was about civilizing the savages. It was about Europeans who are their "elder" brothers making them part of the civilized world, a world in which reason reigns over emotion and fact over fiction. Africans were doomed unless they became subjects of European imperialism. In other words, Africans were considered to be an irreligious lot of unenlightened persons. They were considered as pagans and the unconverted individuals who lack knowledge of God or the Bible. They were neither Jews nor Christians, or even Muslims for that matter.

In the word "pagan", we hear echoes of a people or community professing a polytheistic religion, like the ancient Romans, Greeks, etc. We also find the idea of a backward individual who lives in a village or rural district. And so "pagan" is used by urban elites in the derogatory sense of "peasant" or a person of the countryside, as we, in contemporary parlance, might say "bumpkin" or "hick", indicating one who lacks the "sophistication" of the cities. Yet Africans were seen not only as pagans or heathen; they were to be treated like small children.

Christianity came to be seen by Hegelians as the universal instrument par excellence for civilizing others because it was the highest manifestation of the subjective spirit. It was this spirit of brutality at the time of the Berlin conference that generated the necessary enthusiasm for conquest. It was to be a military and economic triumph, which would leave the permanent scourge of slavery and colonialism that still stares deep into the conscience of Europeans and their descendants. As Aimé Cesaire explains:

> A civilization that proves incapable of solving the problems it creates is a decadent civilization. A civilization that closes its eyes to its most crucial problems is a stricken civilization. A civilization that uses its principles of trickery and deceit is a dying civilization. The fact is that the so-called European civilization as it has been shaped by two centuries of bourgeois rule is incapable of solving two major problems to which its existence has given rise: the problem of the proletariat and the colonial problem; that Europe is unable to justify itself either before the bar of "reason" or before the bar of "conscience".
>
> In Emmanuel Chukwudi Eze ed., *African Philosophy*, p.222

The fundamental historical problem with the European conscience arises from compulsive behaviour with regard to commodification. At the core of this, as argued elsewhere in this book, is the heartless spirit of insatiable capital accumulation even at the expense of human dignity.

Luther and Calvin succeeded in fashioning a new ethical statement for the West which was more in accord with the internal dynamics of European culture. The doctrines that they developed supported the competitive, individualistic, aggressive, rationalistic, non-spiritual and detached behaviour necessary for survival within the culture. There was no longer a question of emulating the New Testament portrait of Jesus.

Most social historians would agree that Protestantism became a religion of the merchant emerging from medieval feudalistic society. Max Weber describes what he calls the bearers of 16th-century Western culture as he relates the "Protestant ethic" to the "spirit of capitalism" in his attempt to demonstrate the influence of certain religious ideas on the development of an economic spirit, or the ethos, of an economic system. In this case, we are dealing with the connection of the spirit of modern economic life with the rational ethics of ascetic Protestantism.

"Capitalism", as the renowned neo-positivist Ayn Rand claims, has "never had a moral base in this country [USA]... there is a fundamental contradiction between capitalism and altruistic morality – capitalism demands the pursuit of one's own interests" (quoted in Marimba, *Yurugu*, p.382). This is a classic and profound critique of the origins and spirit of modern capitalism which is inherent in the selfish nature of European culture. While making claims of universal suffrage and the legitimacy of protest against oppressive regimes in its own backyard, European colonialism never applied its noble democratic ideals during the brutal conquest of foreign lands. So the "colonial Jesus" was part of the strategy for pacifying revolt against the capitalist interests of the imperial regimes. As the Mau Mau freedom fighters in Kenya once said, "When the white man came he had the Bible and we had the land. He told us to close our eyes and pray. When we opened our eyes, he had the land and we had the Bible!"

Story-telling and pedagogy

Beyond historicism, there are aspects of the gospels that appeal to the demands of faith. One cannot simply ignore the radical connotations of the gospel by claiming to know "a Jesus of faith". When peasants read texts about the life of

Jesus, they may read them as if they provide simple details of actual historical events, yet the texts may not automatically provide much-needed experiential understanding. This understanding can be achieved only by connecting to the pedagogic value of the message contained in the life of Jesus. How is the story of a man who is said to have lived two thousand years ago in Palestine, who never walked beyond a tightly circumscribed region, relevant to people living under the yoke of globalized oppression in modern times? The key issue is not so much the historicity of the narrative but its connection with the experiences of struggling people's daily life and how that story becomes part of their own narrative. The meaning given to the Jesus event then becomes relational and not merely rational. Even history is hollow and devoid of content so long as it is derivative of empirical records that do not communicate relational values.

Let us examine an ancient legend from a tribe in West Africa with a perspective on "historical" episodes quite different from that of European civilization. This story, like the written gospels, has its own unique eschatology value and may be referred to as "canonical" for the Akan people of Ghana.

The story, as told by Basil Davidson, goes thus: Once upon a time in the deep forests of West Africa, there lived very peaceful clans of a people known as the Akan. At one point in time, these groups begun to suffer under the authority of other clans (also Akan) to whom they were obliged to pay tribute. If only they could unite and put their rivalries aside, the clans might find a way of regaining the state of bliss that once brought wealth and health to their community. There came to them a man named Agyei who had an impressive reputation for, in living among their strong neighbours, he had acquired spiritual insights and power. They welcomed him and named him Okomfo Ankye; that means in the Twi language of the Akan "a priest and guardian of the ancestral shrines". In addition, his mission was agreed: to unite the Akan people against their neighbours. Word got out among the Akan clans through their leading man, King Osei Tutu.

Tutu, clearly well briefed, called a great gathering of chiefs and elders and queen mothers, even though these events occurred before the Akan gave great value to the influence of women.

The king summoned the court under a great tree and there, as local memory recalls, the priest drew upon his spiritual powers and brought down from the sky, in a black cloud among rumblings and air thick with white dust, a wooden stool with three supports and partly covered with gold. It was in fact a stool of the kind upon which leading Akan sat in council or, at other times, in everyday circumstances. The multitude that day watched in silence as this golden stool descended and rested beside their king. It is said the stool contained the soul and spirit of the Asante nation including their power, health, bravery and welfare. The stool was never to be sat upon by anyone, not even the king or the priest. It was not to be seized by any hostile group, much less destroyed for, if that ever happened, the Asante nation would become sick and die.

The moral of this story is that the golden stool itself represented something unique that could not belong to any living person. That which contains the essence of life cannot be commodified because it comprehends the totality of human experience. No human experience, not even of "history", can fathom in its entirety the depth and meaning this legendary event had for the Akan people. We cannot say there was an event which took place in the distant past, or how accurately it was described, but there is a more important issue than whether that fabled event may or may not have happened.

The story is what keeps the community together and ensures their survival in the event of conflicts or crises of any kind. The meaning is that people may choose presidents or prime ministers to preside or arbitrate in the affairs of the community, but not without accountability to something larger than themselves. In the spirit of the quest for the historical Jesus, what was described by the Akan was internal protest against institutions that had lost their legitimacy and authority. In the same way, later Europeans went to the

Enlightenment to regain a sense of individual authority in the face of feudal structures in Europe. In the case of the African story, the meaning is still being fulfilled in the context of community.

It is the community that gives legitimacy to whoever governs on its behalf. However, the community together with those chosen to preside over its affairs will be held ultimately accountable to what the golden stool represents, that is, a deep spirituality that we seem to have lost but one that we must recover as part of our African heritage. Bénézet Bujo, a scholar of religions and philosophy from the Democratic Republic of Congo, has made this observation: the assertion that the king or the chief was not an absolute ruler is proven by the fact that a council of elders supported him, and without its counsel the ruler did not take critical decisions. On all decisions of public importance, he had to consult this council. The council of elders consisted of sages, very often including women, who were known and recognized, and their moral standard was taken into consideration since they were expected to lead an exemplary life. In addition, every leader was to be endowed with integrity and spirituality, for ultimately all sentient beings were accountable to God.

> While the Jesus Seminar depicts Jesus as an eschatological prophet, as passive revolutionary, as member of the Qumran sect, as proto-Pharisee, as gay magician, as charismatic renewer, as mystic teacher, as Cynic sage, the combination of inflated claims and conflicting results should alone alert serious historians to a fundamental problem.
>
> Ari Marimba, *Yurugu*, p.203

Not only historians but those who are deeply rooted in traditions of sagacity find fault with such scholarship. For Jesus, by virtue of the things said about him and the innocent death that he died in pursuing the highest good for humanity, is the greatest among the sages and is worthy to be named not just one among the many ancestors. His life and ministry show that he could not be just an ordinary being. Let us call him Proto-Ancestor; i.e., God's emissary to the Ancestors.

For Africans ancestors actually exist and appear in dreams, and sometimes they give visible signs to show that they exist. They are no longer historical beings as such, but their existence continues to be manifested historically in the memory of the living. It is the same with Jesus: we continue to know more and more about him because of the things we continuously encounter as part of his historical reality.

In Africa, the democratic paradigm does not exclude God as did the European Enlightenment, nor is it silent on the moral and spiritual dimensions of good governance. True democratic transformation and practice in African society goes hand in hand with spirituality. Here I refer to spirituality in its deepest sense of meaning – not just pious religiosity – because only then does it carry with it new possibilities for an integral and genuinely holistic approach to human life. For Africans, it is the close connection between human experience and structures or systems that yields an integrated understanding of the value of life. The various belief systems and institutions of sage philosophy in Africa remind us that we live in a moral universe nurtured by the web of life-giving and life-sustaining relationships among all beings that inhabit the earth including the ancestral spirits. Life cannot be commodified, nor is it subject to the logic of the market.

The web of relationships in the human community is preserved under the care and nourishment of institutions of affection such as the family, which includes by and large what may be referred to as extended households which guarantee social and cultural continuity. At the heart of this moral cosmology is the principle of participation. It is this vision of interdependent participation that creates structures of inclusivity and hospitality that make life whole. It is through participation that the dignity of every individual is affirmed. To be is to participate. Exclusion from meaningful participation in matters that vitally affect one's life renders one a nonperson.

This integrated understanding of interdependent participation is consistent with the relational value we attach to human events. The functionality of those events is dependent on the quality of relationships and values transmitted in their retelling. How could the vision of Jesus bring about a society that is deeply divided and segregated? The inclusion and caring of Jesus call forth a society in which even the most vulnerable in the community will have his or her dignity respected and affirmed.

At the market-place

In our view *sokoni* provides the space within which this offering is possible (in Kiswahili, *sokoni* means literally "at the market-place"). It is not unrelated to the "public square". But the concept of the market here is the traditional African market. In 1997, *sokoni* was used as the theme of the WCC's Justice, Peace and Creation conference on theology of life which was held in Nairobi. It symbolizes the totality of community life and space. In the context of *sokoni* the church's social capital is to be offered to the most vulnerable in the society. *Sokoni* is a place of memory and a space of contemporary action. It is the common ground and means through which an alternative vision of life may be realized. *Sokoni* in itself is not an ideology, neither is it just a market-place where people go to shop for new ideas.

Unlike virtual space, *sokoni* is real. Parallels may be drawn between cyber-markets or cyber-space (non-physical space), but the symbolism of the village market is not a space of chaos – with uncoordinated, uncontrolled, random flow of information. It is not confined to those who can afford computers and have the technical know-how of fishing out information. It is the sanctuary of life, the place of dialogue with past and future where new ideas are born.

In *sokoni*, Africa is again called to learn the value and art of dialogue, a way of speech and action that brings peace and builds new relationships that can facilitate "win-win" situations. It is a space to visualize, reclaim and reconstruct authentic community with new skills and instruments of social analysis. In other words, *sokoni* is the space for radical expression of the search for an alternative vision that could save not only Africa but the whole world. In relating what is good, the capacity for hope is regained and faith in life is reaffirmed. Here the centre and the periphery and the margin may be redefined.

Sokoni offers a new way of thinking and doing theology. It is the arena through which theoretical discourse becomes *palaver*, an historical event, which touches people's hearts and transforms their understanding of the world. In a way, *sokoni* provides space for paradigm shifts in which the logic of the global system is questioned and redefined. In this regard, a new spirituality is gained that is broader and deeper than mysticism, piety or religiosity because it is centred on the intrinsic value of life itself.

Where do human beings in modern times, be it in Africa or elsewhere, find consolation, meaning and fulfilment of their existence? Where are the sanctuaries? In liturgical or ecclesial terms, could *sokoni* be the place where human beings come to lament, proclaim, elaborate on the theology and ethic of life? Is *sokoni* not a place full of the historical and political memory of the people who are custodians of the resources (earth, air, trees and the spirits) bequeathed to them by God through their ancestors? Is it not a place where we are all invited to seek justice and find peace in one another?

Sokoni is not a building, but a place full of people drawn together by the unifying force of Christ. It is a place in which life abounds in plenty and people are happy not because of what they have but because of what they give and receive as a community.

Sokoni is a real event in the real lives of real people called into critical dialogue with life itself. And as a market it is not just a space filled with goods and enterprises. *Sokoni* is also a sanctuary, a place where history is constantly being made. It has become for us the rebirth and renewal of the human spirit. Doing theology in the market-place of life and in the presence of the community encourages one to bridge the gap between reflection and action. The world is full of markets, and so *sokoni* can be found everywhere; therefore, theology can be done everywhere and at all times!

Sokoni is not just a physical market open to the traffic of goods. *Sokoni* is ecu-space, an ecumenical space and sanctuary of ideas. The concept itself is part of the process of paradigm shift, an authentic alternative vision of life not just for Africa but for the world.

That is also the essence of the World Council of Churches' Special Focus on Africa Programme as a contribution to the reconstruction of Africa. We are called not just to react, or be reactionaries, to the plight of Africa. We must not deplore Africa's present in terms of its marginality and human sadness that come with war and the anguish of poverty. We must not forever remain infected by nostalgic memories of the past in our desperation for solutions, nor can we resort to the rigour of historicism lest we become victims of ideological fatigue characterizing the end of an era. Rather, we must regard the recurrent problems in our world as an invitation to a new moment of enthusiasm (*enthusiasmos* = "God" within us coming to life) which will bring to birth a new spirit coming first from Africa and then being offered to the rest of the world.

Sokoni must provide the space and opportunity for a new and lasting incarnation of the spirit so that those who are "infected" by it can spread the necessary enthusiasm for a new life to begin. *Sokoni* has the potential to become a space full of life-giving resources, a place where the goodness of life itself sanctifies our memory and connection with history.

11. Fighting Poverty

Fundamental to a new vision for a better Africa is the struggle to eradicate poverty. Not merely to alleviate it, but to eradicate it. Others may be content with alleviation or reduction of poverty. For Africans, our goal should be to eradicate poverty because this goal is noble, and it is the right course to chart and pursue.

It is also possible. The resources are there, the technical ability is there, it is now a question of political will. It is, therefore, an ethical question as well. When a small group of Africans announced in Manchester, England, in 1945 that Africa would be free, it was considered a big joke. African peasants and workers to take on the mighty British empire – impossible! But fully equipped with kindred spirit, political will and fierce determination, they returned to their respective countries and initiated liberation movements. The rest is history. Later, when Ian Smith as prime minister of Rhodesia said, "not in a thousand years", he was completely serious. That was in 1975, when Smith could not imagine how the Zimbabwe Chemurenga could possibly defeat the well trained and well endowed Rhodesian forces. Barely five years later, colonial Rhodesia became independent Zimbabwe. Apartheid was considered not just a social construct by white South Africa but it was believed that it had divine sanction as well. So the architects of apartheid held that anybody opposed to it was working against God's will.

The colonizers made vain attempts to redirect the process of liberation struggles. They suggested reforms and adjustments here and there, but that did not deter the resolve of Africans to achieve freedom at any cost. Nor did it blur the vision of independence for the whole of Africa. The same zeal is now required with respect to fighting poverty. The motivation should flow from righteous indignation cherished by those who consider abject poverty to be no less repugnant than enslavement and colonial subjugation.

Following the end of political colonialism in Africa, it is now imperative for Africans to come up with a new vision: a new vision for liberating Africa and the Africans from the abyss of poverty and its dehumanizing consequences. This calls not only for economic and industrial prudence but for intellectual and spiritual profundity as well. Economic emancipation must be accompanied by spiritual emancipation. The African human condition is more than just material deprivation. The mistake made at independence was to consider political emancipation an end in itself.

Eradication of poverty must be comprehensive and multi-faceted, involving concerted efforts at all levels. While the primary responsibility lies with Africans themselves, external support and solidarity are expected to accompany African initiatives. This is the case especially for Europe which, after all, contributed immensely to the impoverishment of Africa. But the external contribution and involvement must be viewed critically. The paradigms, methodologies and language used should not be taken at face value. The process must be evaluated at its different stages to ensure clarity at the levels of concept, policy and implementation.

The fight against poverty should start from the vantage point of the poor themselves, especially as regards their consciousness of their social and economic conditions. At the dawn of the 21st century, we witness an epic unfolding at the grassroots. The poor are overcoming their longstanding oppressed consciousness as they attain a liberated consciousness. That does not mean they are no longer oppressed, but by speaking their own language and charting their own course they are claiming the right not to be oppressed and asserting their human rights, including social and economic rights.

This is a huge step in the struggle against poverty; only two decades ago, the poor looked to benevolence to deliver them from their condition. As recently as the 1970s and 1980s, many among the poor resigned themselves to their fate of being powerless and voiceless and considered themselves at the mercy of the powerful. The powerful, for their part, were successful in keeping the poor perpetually in their place through oppressive social, political and economic structures.

Any concept is open to misuse as long as it is not clearly linked to practices of solidarity, or the culture of sharing. Concepts are subject to interpretation and may easily be co-opted. This has been the case with the concept and language of development. For instance, language that developed among social movements working for people-centred development was in time co-opted by the World Bank, G8 governments and other powerful actors, giving new meaning to the terms. Clear evidence of this is observed in the language used in the documents of the UN Social Summit in Copenhagen in 1995. Poverty alleviation, people as the subject, empowering the poor and capacity-building are fast being adopted as mainstream language in the development discourse.

When everybody seems to subscribe to the same goals and the same values in development policy, it is necessary carefully and critically to examine the operative values that guide implementation. If the operative values are guided by the neo-liberal economic model and its idolatry of the so-called free market, then market mechanisms become the means of implementation. However, these means contradict the stated goals. The more international financial institutions have been involved in poverty alleviation, the more poverty has increased. Konrad Raiser of the World Council of Churches put it very well when he said the policies of these institutions

> ...have not only failed to bridge the gap between rich and poor and achieve greater equality, but rather contributed to a widening gap – the virtual exclusion of an increasing number of the poor and widespread social disintegration. The OECD, comprised exclusively of rich countries, can hardly be said to have the interests of the poor nations at the centre of its concerns.

> Konrad Raiser in a letter of June 2000
> to UN secretary-general Kofi Annan

The Social Summit in Copenhagen in 1995 made a significant step in addressing the issue of poverty in at least two respects. It recognized the critical need for dealing with both the complexity and the simplicity of concepts. By acknowledging that global poverty cannot be fully understood without seeing it in the context of historical, economic, political, social and cultural issues, it admitted the structural nature of poverty and the linkages of its causes. By agreeing on a baseline measure of poverty, that is $1.00 per day, it gave a simple indicator to help in monitoring progress of the poverty alleviation process. Secondly, the summit placed emphasis on the donor-receiver partnership as a critical aspect of the vision of poverty alleviation. (It should be noted that partnership as a concept and language had been written into the ecumenical development agenda of the World Council of Churches since the early 1970s.)

A quick assessment of the progress made since the Copenhagen summit reveals that much remains to be done. The summit had as its main target reducing by half the incidence of dollar-poor by 2015. With more than a quarter of the target period over, what has been achieved remains unimpressive. Only China seems to be on target, having reduced the incidence of dollar-poor from 29.4 percent to 17.2 percent. In East and South Asia, the reduction is a mere 2.3 percent, (from 28.5 to 26.2 percent). In sub-Saharan Africa, by and large, the growth has been too small to indicate poverty has been affected.

This shows that unless an economic miracle occurs in the near future, poverty alleviation by 2015 will, once again, elude the development designers. Before the failure of the "development decades" became obvious, the dynamics of being poor were such that the oppressed poor finally accepted the inhumanity and humiliation of their situation. They accepted the status quo as the normal course of life.

Listening to the world's poor

But this situation is changing fast because the people at the grassroots are seeking to go beyond the premises of modernity. They are reinventing and creating afresh their own intellectual and institutional frameworks without necessarily getting sucked into the power disputes of the elite. This process of liberating themselves from the dominant ideologies has enhanced their dignity, and they are finally being listened to. Far from "being empowered" by the rich and powerful, the poor are becoming self-empowering.

The lived experiences of the poor give legitimacy to the language and categories they use in telling their stories. The poor are by no means a monolithic group. They are diverse because their social contexts are diverse; they are rooted in their local soils, their local spaces and cultures. Yet the diversity is not a source of conflict. Rather, it is a source of mutual inspiration, as we have witnessed when the poor are linked together.

A good example is what the WCC witnesses when indigenous peoples from different parts of the world attend meetings or are involved in exchange visits. There is a high level of resonance in their stories and life testaments. They bond naturally as they realize how wide a ground they have in common. As Gustavo Esteva and Madhu Suri Prakash relate, in sharing life with life, the indigenous peoples discover and "reveal a multiplicity of different cosmic visions conceived at the local level, emerging from the ruins left by modernity. After 'the end of History', we can have the continuation and regeneration of thousands of histories."

One way the ecumenical movement can accompany the poor in their struggles is by providing safe spaces for them to share images and metaphors, concepts and words capable of revealing what is emerging as people gain confidence in their ability to generate solutions to their problems. Secondly, we can provide the networks for sharing more widely the postmodern ethos of liberation that transcends the mechanical way of spreading the neo-liberal prescriptions for alleviating poverty. Esteva and Prakash could not have put it better when they argue:

> Post-modernity already exists where people refuse to be seduced and controlled by economic laws. It exists for peoples rediscovering and reinventing their traditional commons by re-embedding the economy (to use Polanyi's expression) into society and culture; subordinating it again to politics and ethics;

marginalizing it – putting it at their margins; which is precisely what it means to be a "marginal" in modern times.

Gustavo Esteva and Madhu Suri Prakash,
Grassroots Post-Modernism, pp.133 and 194.

By affirming the poor in their search for home-grown solutions to their problems, the church facilitates them in recovering their sense of well-being and in rediscovering motives for their renewed hopes of liberation despite the hope they lost in fruitless pursuit of the prescriptions provided by the failed development designer.

These reflections are by no means intended to romanticize or idealize poor people and poverty. They are a recognition of new awareness among the poor and concomitant, emerging paradigms. Life is still very hard for them, yet the poor have decided against being fatalistic. The findings of Project 21 on "Christianity, Poverty and Wealth" provide very rich materials on the reality as seen through the eyes of the poor (*Project 21: Christianity, Poverty and Wealth* is a project of Heads of Agencies Network, HoAN. Its findings have been published by the WCC; see bibliography, Taylor). The method of case studies helps to authenticate the language and categories used in this report. The report introduces voices of the poor from different parts of the world. It is a significant contribution to ecumenical thinking and suggests ways of fighting poverty in the 21st century.

Perhaps the most powerful illustration of the growing strength and inspiration derived from networking is expressed by the presence in Ramallah, Palestine, of representatives of the international peasant movement Via Campesina. Their leaders from the landless movement of Brazil and farmers union of the Basque (between Spain and France) were among the 35 internationals who defied the Israeli military blockade on 30 March 2002 and met Yasser Arafat in his besieged headquarters at Ramallah. They added their voice to those urging "all governments to raise the pressure on the Israeli government by sending their consuls and representatives to Ramallah".

Globalization from below

The WCC Indigenous Peoples Programme and the Special Focus on Africa are examples of new ways of accompaniment and specific expressions of solidarity with the poor. The programmes were born out of the Canberra and Harare assemblies (1991 and 1998). In both cases, the indigenous peoples and Africans called on the WCC to look at their situations with "new eyes" and move beyond words. They did not ask the WCC for handouts but invited the ecumenical movement to accompany them in their "journey of hope". In these cases, the main role of the WCC is, with regard to the indigenous peoples, "...to support the struggles of the racially oppressed peoples and communities for dignity, identity and justice"; and with regard to Africans, to "galvanize churches, ecumenical organizations/networks and specialized bodies inside Africa into concerted action towards realizing Africa's journey of hope, and to enable African churches to provide leadership in spirituality and economic emancipation of the continent". In both cases, the overall goal is to promote life with dignity in just and sustainable communities.

Instead of corporate globalization "liberalizing" trade and finances in favour of transnational corporations and the powerful actors in the financial markets, there is need for globalization of people-centred alternatives, a globalization from below. This was on the agenda of the social movements and churches which participated in the World Social Forum at Porto Alegre, Brazil, in April 2002. They demonstrated their dignity by stating, "We are here in spite of the attempts to break our solidarity. We come together again to continue our struggles against neo-liberalism and war, to confirm the agreements of the last forum and to reaffirm that another world is possible."

The movements assert that their diversity is their strength; in other words, dignity is found in the recognition of diversity. The social movements' statement continued, "We are diverse – women and men, adults and youth, indigenous peoples, rural and urban, workers and unemployed, homeless, the elderly, students, professionals, peoples of every creed, colour and sexual orientation. The expression of this diversity is our strength and the basis of our unity." Dignity is also seen in people's solidarity and determination to fight repressive systems. "We are a global solidarity movement, united in our determination to fight against the concentration of wealth, the proliferation of poverty and inequalities, and the destruction of our earth." Again, dignity is complete if the earth is treated with dignity. The social movements are working for alternatives which reaffirm human dignity and that of the earth by resisting systems that destroy people's dignity.

The HIV/AIDS pandemic and its devastating impact is by far the most formidable challenge in the struggle against poverty today. Its toll, particularly in sub-Saharan Africa, has reached plague proportions and is still rising. But even in this area those infected, as well as those affected, have decided not to give up. The words of Gideon Byamugisha, himself HIV-positive, best sum up the increasing resilience of those infected (see epigraph to ch. 8). His statement is a powerful affirmation of the human dignity of those living with HIV/AIDS.

The newly established ecumenical HIV/AIDS initiative in Africa is a good model of how the church could enter into meaningful solidarity with the poor. This initiative brings together churches and church-related organizations in Africa; churches, ecumenical and church-related organizations in Europe and North America; and the World Council of Churches, in concerted efforts to respond to the challenges posed by HIV/AIDS. In addition to providing financial support, the ecumenical funding agencies acknowledge that, "The gravity of the HIV/AIDS epidemic has helped to expose the systemic issues that foster social injustice and inequality, and multiply the loss of life to AIDS: violence and conflict, poverty, unjust trading practices, debt and gender inequality."

Fighting poverty has a number of essential elements, the first of which should be affirming the right of the poor to liberate themselves from their human condition: the struggle against oppression and for liberation. This has been the approach of social movements, for whom the fight against poverty was, and still is, essentially a class struggle and an anti-racist struggle. In their participation in this struggle, women bring a new dimension. Gender analysis has introduced the notion of the feminization of poverty, thus enriching discernment in regard to the struggle against poverty. Fighting poverty, then, means a fight of the poor and by the poor for their own liberation. The term "fighting poverty" has its origin in the analysis of poverty and impoverishment which includes the social and political dimensions of society. The struggle to change this material condition does, therefore, assume social and political dimensions. Poverty was not first of all defined as a deficit of people, but as a social location, as something that marks the space and place of social actors. Social actors, communities of struggle, systemic injustice, structural violence, solidarity and change are critical elements that must characterize the struggle to eradicate poverty.

When the poor as social actors begin to disappear behind poverty as defined by the statistics of the international financial institutions like the World Bank, our whole understanding changes. Now poverty becomes an abstract term, a deficiency of socially disabled and weak individuals which can be described in terms of access to the dollar, a problem that has to be repaired by society through certain means at the disposal of the society. This shift of emphasis destroys the continuum between ends and means and runs the risk of reducing the problem to something that can be addressed by market means. The actors become invisible, both the poor and those responsible for the mechanisms of impoverishment in an unjust system. The excessive accumulation of wealth by the rich is no longer seen so much as a root cause, but rather, the wealth of the rich is portrayed as the basis for a solution, as the shining example, a pathway that people should follow.

At this point, fighting poverty becomes a weak, co-opted and misleading concept, legitimizing and defending the status quo.

The public discourse on poverty alleviation is completely dominated by this approach; that is to say, the focus has been put on economic growth through trade and finances (which is at the centre of the discourse on economic globalization), and anything else becomes secondary to this. This is the main reason why a new language is needed, a new language spoken not by the non-poor but by the poor themselves. The challenge of the church is to develop the capacity to listen, hear and understand what the poor are saying. It is only then that we can be seen to affirm the poor in their struggle for the right to self-determination.

An issue of justice

The second essential element is to advocate fighting poverty by making it a justice issue. This is not a new insight in the ecumenical movement. The WCC fifth assembly in Nairobi in 1975 said:

> Poverty, we are learning, is caused primarily by unjust structures that leave the resources and the power to make decisions about the utilization of resources in the hands of a few within nations and among nations... Unjust structures are often the consequence of wrong or misdirected goals and values.

David Paton ed., *Breaking Barriers*, p.123

It is a sign of life when the poor, the marginalized and the excluded everywhere stand up to resist unjust powers and structures and forge their own destiny. In these processes, the poor have learned to reject any justification – social, religious or ethnic – for their condition. By and large, the majority of the poor in the world today are impoverished by the structures and systems of injustice. They as a people did not just start poor. They were made poor, and history is the unbiased witness to this reality: the indigenous peoples in the Americas and Australia; the disinherited Africans on the continent of Africa and in the diaspora; the untouchables and dalits of India – all these peoples have been impoverished by processes of colonialism and enslavement. Their plight has been aggravated by unjust trade and economic globalization whose logic further excludes them from the mainstream economies.

The more the ecumenical movement participates in expressing its solidarity with the poor and the excluded in their struggles, the clearer the interlinkages among various manifestations of injustice and oppression become. Racism, sexism, class domination, the denial of peoples' rights, casteism, all are inter-linked and woven together like a spider's web. Singly and together, they are at the root of many injustices which cause much suffering, misery, poverty and death. The instruments of oppression which maintain and sustain this web vary from the subtle smile of denial to mammoth military machines.

The WCC's Vancouver assembly in 1983 considered spirituality to constitute an important element in the church's expression of solidarity with the poor. An excerpt reads:

> churches [should] explore forms through which Christian spirituality is manifest in the struggle for justice and human dignity. For this purpose, we call churches to cultivate and strengthen the spiritual life among the people, through prayer, Bible study and worship, making justice and human dignity an integral part of the churches' life.

David Gill ed., Gathered for Life, p.89

Spirituality for liberation is important when poverty is considered to have not only material consequences for the poor, but also brings humiliation which greatly violates their dignity. What the poor demand of the society is not charity but justice, and a socio-economic environment that allows for its realization.

Fighting poverty by naming the conditions of the poor as intolerable in our time adds a new insight which must not be lost on the ecumenical agenda in the 21st century. The greatest scandal of our age is that, amidst the unprecedented wealth of nations and individuals, millions of people have sunk below acceptable levels of poverty. The corresponding disparities between the excessively rich and the massively poor are equally unprecedented.

In 1960, the poorest 20 percent of the world's people received 2.3 percent of global income. By 1991, their share had sunk to 1.4 percent. Today, the poorest 20 percent receive only 1.1 percent of global income. The ratio of income of the wealthiest 20 percent of the people to that of the poorest 20 percent was 30 to 1 in 1960. By 1995, that ratio stood at 82 to 1. The 20 percent of the world's people who live in the highest-income countries account for 86 percent of total worldwide private consumption expenditures; the poorest 20 percent, only 1.3 percent. These global disparities are mirrored within many countries. In Brazil, for example, the poorest 50 percent of the population received 18 percent of the national income in 1960, falling to 11.6 percent in 1995. The richest ten percent of Brazilians received 54 percent of national income in 1960; by 1995 this proportion had risen to 63 percent.

Kim Jim Yong, Joyce V. Millen, Alec Irwin
and John Gershman eds, Dying for Growth, p.14

Something is gravely wrong when at the beginning of the 21st century the wealth of the three richest individuals on earth surpassed the combined annual GDP of the 48 least developed countries. While every day millions of tons of food are wasted, some 840 million people sleep hungry.

The UNDP's human development report of 1998 shows that the 15 richest individuals in the world enjoy combined assets that exceed the total annual GDP of sub-Saharan Africa. Meanwhile, over a billion people in the world lack access to clean water, and 1.2 billion people lack adequate housing. What these comparisons show is that the world does have sufficient resources to lift up the dollar-poor of the world from their present conditions.

But the world lacks the will and the ways of implementing a just system that will allocate and distribute available resources.

For technical and statistical purposes, poverty is usually measured by establishing a poverty line, set at some multiple of the income necessary to purchase a basic food basket that provides sufficient nutrition for an active, productive life. People whose income is below the level necessary to purchase even that basic food basket are called absolutely poor, or in deprivation. A significant degree of arbitrariness is involved in setting poverty lines. The World Bank has established a line for absolute poverty at $1 per day, as measured by relative purchasing power parity. Using this line means there are 1.3 billion people living in absolute poverty. If the World Bank had used a line of $2 per day, the figure would be 3 billion. At whatever level the line is set, the number of people who fall below the line is called the headcount index, usually represented as a percentage of the population.

Dying for Growth, p.15.

With such a huge number of people living in absolute poverty, the fight against poverty cannot be left to neo-liberal mechanical ways of poverty alleviation. As shown earlier, that strategy is not working anyway.

Poverty should be included in the continuum of "intolerable" conditions in history: slavery, colonialism, apartheid. There comes a time in the history of humanity when a plight becomes so morally and spiritually repugnant that the greater part of humanity rises up to struggle against it. In the 21st century, abject poverty has reached such depth that it should be considered a grievous crime to allow such a situation to prevail when resources and means exist to prevent it.

Constitutional protections

The International Bill of Rights recognized long ago that poverty and human rights are intimately related. But the development of social and cultural rights lags far behind that of civil and political rights. This has to do with the fact that the victims of violations of the former are generally the poor, while the victims of the latter are by and large relatively well educated and materially well to do. In more recent times, human-rights advocates have been discussing more seriously the possibility of making violations of economic and social rights crimes against humanity.

In 2000, the UNDP launched the rights-approach "as a new paradigm for finding innovative and integrative strategies to tackle poverty and other violations of basic human dignity". But, as Bas de Gaay Fortman argues, limiting the issues at the "rights" level alone is not enough because "a right implies neither more nor less than legal protection of freedoms and entitlements, and hence an abstract acknowledgment of claims based on these". It is only when a right is lifted to the level of entitlement that it becomes concrete; and it becomes an actual acquisition when it is recognized as a claim. It is therefore imperative that legal frameworks be found to enable the poor to lay claims on the society on account of violations of their basic rights.

As of now, such frameworks and mechanisms are not in place for most countries in Africa. But for the states whose constitutions include a bill of rights and the legal mechanisms to implement them, it is possible to identify the duty-bearer against whom claims could be made. A good example, mentioned by Fortman, is South Africa, where the constitutional court ruled in October 2000 in favour of Grootboom and 899 other destitute squatters. The ruling obliged the government to provide alternative shelter for the squatters whose shelter had been demolished because they were deemed illegal occupants. This is a case where housing is considered a basic right, and redress was possible because it is entrenched in the constitution. But unlike South Africa's, the constitutions of most African countries do not provide a bill of rights that includes food, health and shelter as basic human rights; where they do, as in the case of Kenya, the judiciary system has been so disabled that it lacks the clout for effective implementation. It is therefore crucially important that we advocate that all African countries write a bill of rights into their constitutions. That way, constitutional and legal mechanisms will exist providing the basis for the poor to lay claims for their basic rights.

If the newly established African Union were to accord the highest priority to fighting poverty, then all heads of state individually and collectively would have to be seen to make efforts towards that goal. They should hold each other accountable for their work towards eradication of poverty in their respective states, and concomitantly in Africa as a whole. All should be challenged to establish a baseline for measuring efforts made towards the goal of poverty eradication. The baseline could be set using the Copenhagen definition of abject poverty; i.e. living on one dollar per day.

As demonstrated above, this is not the most desirable way of determining poverty, but so far it is the best standard we have in terms of a measurable and verifiable method. To show the seriousness of the government efforts at poverty eradication, an independent commission could be set up to monitor the progress made by the heads of state. The commission could issue annual reports including state-by-state assessments on the efforts and progress made. Of course, natural calamities like severe drought or floods should be taken into account. The best performing head of state could be honoured while the poorest would be exposed.

Other actors should not be let off the hook. At the international level, ways and mechanisms could be established to identify institutions or governments which have contributed to poverty growth in Africa. Objective criteria must be set up against which an institution or state is to be assessed and found culpable. An example could be identifying how many households might have been made to slip below the poverty line on account of implementation of policies or programmes of the respective institutions. A shame list of the culpable institutions and/or states could be published for all to see. This could be a step towards recognizing violations of social and economic rights as crimes against humanity.

The role of the poor

The poor themselves play a central role in processes of poverty reduction. They are very resourceful, creative, imaginative, ingenious and, of course, very hard working. Otherwise, they could not survive against the strong odds that militate against their lives on a daily basis. To enable the poor to achieve their potential, it is necessary to build and strengthen local institutions and enable them to network and relate horizontally. Local ownership of these institutions must be emphasized. The goal of such institutions is not merely to attain institutional capacity for its own sake. Rather, it should include the political and social interests represented by these institutions, be they community organizations or social movements.

Social intervention or patronage by external NGOs (indigenous or foreign) must not be allowed to replace the role of the local organizers and leadership. The local groups should be enabled to gain the power capacity to resist any manipulation by politicians who might show a tendency to use the organizations for their own political interests. How decisions are made, and in whose interests, and who runs these institutions, are legitimate questions that need to be examined. Local politics has a dynamic of its own. It consists of more than formal political processes. The pervasiveness of local politics is such that social interactions greatly influence political and economic change in a given locality. But the reality is even more complex because of the multiplicity of factors that constantly interact in the processes of decision making. Neil Webster and Lars Engberg-Pedersen have correctly observed that

> local politics encompasses many spheres and touches upon questions of religion, ethnicity, market structures and so on. The basis of influence and legitimacy, as well as of political struggle itself, are to be found both inside and outside formal political institutions.

> Neil Webster and Lars Engberg-Pedersen eds,
> *In the Name of the Poor*, p.21

That means the political space is of crucial importance in fighting poverty. Affirming the poor in their roles will be greatly enhanced by having in place strong local institutions owned and run by local people themselves. These institutions should not be single-issue groups but must have a holistic approach to problems. It is important also that their membership be inclusive.

Upholding the dignity of all human beings in the society is achievable where sharing of available resources is built into the social fabric. Different societies have different ways and systems of sharing. In the industrialized rich countries, a welfare system alleviates the plight of the unemployed and those with a low income. But with economic globalization and with increasing migration, third-world characteristics have begun to be manifested in many cities in Europe and North America. Today the homeless, beggars and even victims of starvation are not uncommon in many cities of the industrialized world.

We have already shown that in Africa a communitarian ethic provides the framework and mechanisms that make significant sharing possible. The economies of affection will have greater impact and benefit more people if the majority in the community are enabled to participate in generating more wealth. Broadening of economic opportunities and developing effective and efficient infrastructure within and between African countries would be a huge step in that direction. Given that Africa is predominantly rural, increasing food production must be given top priority.

The discourse on food sovereignty is basically about the ability of communities to raise their own food. Food sovereignty includes questions of food security, but the concept of food security as a human right is not clear enough nor is any principle as to how this human right is implemented. There is not a sufficiently realistic critique of an exclusive focus on market means and food aid by the over-producing countries such as the USA and the European Union.

Since food aid does not and cannot lead to food sovereignty, what we need to promote is for the poor to attain self-reliance in food production. It is beneath the dignity of a people to be fed by others, and worse still when those responsible for generating and sustaining the structures of injustice are the ones doing the feeding.

Our critique of the New Partnership for Africa's Development (NEPAD) notwithstanding, we consider the initiative to be an important step in the right direction. The WCC Special Focus on Africa anticipated the urgency and significance of a new vision for Africa when African participants at the Harare assembly in 1998 undertook to reconstruct and rebuild our communities and work tirelessly for a future of Africa full of life in abundance, to continue the unfinished task of transforming our social, political and economic systems and institutions for an inclusive and just society; to seek and pursue peace and reconciliation for our people and communities; and to establish appropriate ethical values in work, governance and management, and good stewardship.

Hence, one cannot over-emphasize the need for church-state dialogue on essential elements of such a vision. The ecumenical organizations and churches in Africa should be assisted in such an engagement.

One of the areas of engagement could be in concerted efforts towards economic emancipation both at the level of discernment (vision) and strategies (especially in fighting poverty). A strong ethical foundation is imperative for good governance to survive and thrive. The Harare covenant referred to ethical and spiritual values that could provide the ingredients for the soul of society and the undergirding of democracy in Africa.

At the level of strategies, the church could offer valuable input by mobilizing its social capital. The church, especially in sub-Saharan Africa, has engaged the people at a profound level. In any given week, Christians from all walks of life interact in congregations and undertake various activities within the communities. By serving and participating in diverse committees and community-based organizations, people have gained civic skills which have deep utility in service to the society. In many rural communities, the church is about the only social institution that people, Christians and non-Christians alike, relate to. It is not uncommon to find that the only health care and medical services available to over sixty percent of the people are those provided by church health clinics and centres. The church occupies a strategic social site and offers a broad network that links the ordinary people in their economic and social activities. Therefore, galvanizing efforts between the church, other faith communities, the civil society and the state would provide resources and release enormous energy towards eradicating poverty in Africa.

By working together towards the same goal of building just, peaceful, sustainable and prosperous communities, the churches and their partners will give the people of Africa the reason to live and find the courage to hope.

Bibliography

Adedeji, Adebayo ed., *South Africa and Africa – Within or Apart?*, Capetown, SADRI, 1996.

Alves, Rubem A., *A Theology of Human Hope*, Washington DC, Corpus, 1969.

Bangura, Zainab, in *New African*, London, IC Publications, Sept. 2001, no. 398, p.38.

Betting on the Weak: Some Experiences in People's Participation in Development, WCC, 1976.

Botemps, Arna, "A Note of Humility", in Abraham Chapman ed., *Black Voices*, New York, Penguin, 1968, p.421.

Bujo, Bénézet, *African Theology in Its Social Context*, Nairobi, Pauline's Publications Africa, 1986.

Bujo, Bénézet, *The Ethical Dimension of Community: The African Model and the Dialogue between North and South*, Nairobi, Pauline's Publications Africa, 1997.

Byamugisha, Gideon, statement at the consultation on ecumenical response to HIV/AIDS in Africa, Nairobi, Kenya, Nov. 2001. See "Plan of Action" adopted at the consultation, http://www.wcc-coe.org/wcc/news/press/01/hiv-aids-plan.html.

Caetano, Marcello, *Os Nativos na Economia Africana*, Cimbre, 1954.

Cesaire, Aimé, in Emmanuel Chudwudi Eze ed., *African Philosophy: An Anthology*, Massachusetts MA, Blackwell, 1998.

Davidson, Basil, *The Black Man's Burden: Africa and the Curse of the Nation State*, Nairobi, East African Educational Publ., 1993, pp.169, 54-56.

Dickinson, Richard D.N. ed., *Economic Globalization: Deepening Challenge for Christians*, WCC, 1998.

Diop, Cheik Anta, *The African Origin of Human Civilization*, Chicago, Chicago Review Press, 1991.

Diop, Cheik Anta, *Black Africa: The Economic and Cultural Basis for a Federated State*, Chicago Review Press, 1987.

Diop, Cheik Anta, *Civilization or Barbarism: An Authentic Anthropology*, New York, Lawrence Hill, 1991.

Diop, Cheik Anta, *Precolonial Black Africa: A Comparative Study of the Political and Social Systems of Europe and Black Africa, from Antiquity to the Formation of Modernity*, New York, Lawrence Hill, 1990.

Dussel, Enrique, *Ethics and the Theology of Liberation*, Maryknoll NY, Orbis, 1978, p.3.

Esteva, Gustavo and Madhu Suri Prakash, *Grassroots Post-Modernism: Remaking the Soil of Cultures*, London, Zed, 1998.

Facing AIDS: The Challenge, the Churches' Response, Geneva, WCC Publications, 1997.

Fanon, Frantz, *The Wretched of the Earth*, New York, Grove, 1963.

Fortman, Bas de Gaay, "Poverty as Human Rights", deficity paper delivered at Tilburg University, 11-13 Oct. 2001, pp.7, 10.

Freire Paulo, *Pedagogy of the Oppressed*, New York, Vintage, 1978. His ethics and methods of participatory pedagogy are of great relevance to a suffering and oppressed people in rural Africa.

Garvey, Marcus, editorial entitled "African Fundamentalism", found at http://www.marcusgarvey.com/african.htm-9k.

Gill, David ed., *Gathered for Life: Official Report, VI Assembly, World Council of Churches*, WCC, 1983.

The Guardian Weekly, 11-17 July 2002, vol. 167.

Hailey, Lord, *An African Survey*, London, OUP, 1936, p.150.

216

Jackson, John G., *Introduction to African Civilizations*, Secaucus NJ, Citadel, 1970, p.305.

Kessler, Diane ed., *Together on the Way: Official Report of the Eighth Assembly of the World Council of Churches*, WCC, 1999.

Kim Jim Yong, Joyce V. Millen, Alec Irwin and John Gershman eds, *Dying for Growth: Global Inequality and the Health of the Poor*, Monroe ME, Common Courage, 2000.

King, Martin Luther Jr, in his sermon "The Most Durable Power", delivered on 6 Nov. 1956 in Montgomery, Alabama.

Kinnamon, Michael, *Signs of the Spirit: Official Report, Seventh Assembly*, WCC, 1991.

Magesa, Laurenti, *African Religion: The Moral Traditions of Abundant Life*, Nairobi, Pauline's Publications Africa, 1997.

Mamdani, Mahmood, *Citizen and Subject: Contemporary Africa and the Legacy of Late Colonialism*, Princeton, Princeton UP, 1996.

Mamdani, Mahmood, *When Victims Become Killers: Colonialism, Nativism, and the Genocide in Rwanda*, Princeton, Princeton UP, 2001.

Mandela, Nelson, *Long Walk to Freedom*, London, Little Brown, 1994.

Marimba, Ari, *Yurugu: An African-Centered Critique of European Cultural Thought and Behaviour*, Asmara, Africa World Press, 1994.

Mazrui, Ali A., *The African Condition*, London, Heinemann, 1982.

Mbeki, Thabo , *Africa – The Time Has Come*, Cape Town, Tafelberg, 1998.

Mollu, Aba, "Christianity and African Traditional Religions: The Case of the Nomadic Pastoralists of Eastern Africa", *Wajibu Magazine*, vol. 4, no. 1, Nairobi, Kenya, 1989.

Mudimbe, V.Y., *The Invention of Africa: Gnosis, Philosophy and the Order of Knowledge*, Bloomington IN, Indiana UP, 1988.

Mugambi, J.N.K. ed., *Democracy and Development in Africa: The Role of Churches*, Nairobi, All Africa Conference of Churches, 1997.

Müller-Fahrenholz, Geiko, *The Art of Forgiveness: Theological Reflections on Healing and Reconciliation*, WCC, 1997.

Musheshe, Mwalimu, in Julius E. Nyang'oro, *Civil Society and Democratic Development in Africa: Perspectives from Eastern and Southern Africa*, Harare, Mwengo, 1999.

Muyale-Manenji, Fridah, "The Effects of Globalization on Culture in Africa in the Eyes of an African Woman", at http://www.wcc-coe.org/wcc/what/jpc/effglob.html.

New African, no. 398, London, IC Publications, July-Aug. 2001.

Nkrumah, Kwame, *Africa Must Unite, Pan-Africanism*, London, Panaf, 1985.

Nyerere, Julius K., 1968, *Freedom and Socialism: A Selection from Writings and Speeches 1965-1967*, Dar es Salaam, Oxford UP, 1999, pp.19-21.

Oliver, Roland, *The African Experience*, London, Phoenix, 1991.

Paton, David ed., *Breaking Barriers: Nairobi 1975*, WCC, 1976.

Raiser, Konrad, *Churches and Transnational Corporations: An Ecumenical Programme*, WCC, 1983.

218

Raiser, Konrad, *Ecumenism in Transition – A Paradigm Shift in the Ecumenical Movement?*, WCC, 1991.

Raiser, Konrad, *For a Culture of Life – Transforming Globalization and Violence*, WCC, 2002.

Raiser, Konrad, *To Be the Church – Challenges and Hopes for a New Millennium*, WCC, 1997.

Raiser, Konrad, letter to UN secretary-general Kofi Annan, 28 June 2000. The letter is a response to a report entitled "A Better World for All" issued jointly by the UN secretary-general with the senior officers of the OECD, the World Bank and the IMF at the opening of "Geneva 2000", the UN special session on development.

Taylor Ian and Williams Paul, in *The Journal of African Affairs*, vol. 100, 2001, London, Royal Africa Society, pp.265-86.

Taylor, Michael, *Christianity, Poverty and Wealth – The Findings of 'Project 21'*, London, Society for Promoting Christian Knowledge, 2003.

Tillich, Paul, *The Courage to Be*, Glasgow, William Collins, 1952.

Webster, Neil and Lars Engberg-Pedersen eds, *In the Name of the Poor: Contesting Political Space for Poverty Reduction*, London, Zed, 2002.

West, Cornel, *Race Matters*, New York, Vintage, 1993.

Wile, David, African Studies Centre, Michigan State University, 1981, on using "tribe" and "tribalism" categories to misunderstand African societies, at http://www.sas.upenn. edu/African_Studies/K-12/Tribe. html-6k.